Celebrating Every Day

Celebrating Every Day

100 EASY RECIPES TO MAKE ANY DAY FEEL SPECIAL

Melissa Johnson *of*

 BEST FRIENDS *for* FROSTING

HARVEST

An Imprint of WILLIAM MORROW

HarperCollins books may be purchased for educational, business, or sales promotional use. For information, please email the Special Markets Department at SPsales@harpercollins.com.

FIRST EDITION

Designed by Melissa Lotfy
Food photography © by Andy Johnson
Lifestyle photography © by Tra Huynh
Illustrations by Nicole Yang
Culinary assistant: Andy Johnson
Prop stylist: Kim Alcala
Wardrobe: Draper James
Hair: Emily Scott, Mai Phuong, and Julia Vorobets
Makeup: Mandie Fenrich and Taryn Passifione

Summer icon © M/stock.adobe.com
Game day icon © GStudio/stock.adobe.com

Library of Congress Cataloging-in-Publication Data has been applied for.

ISBN 978-0-06-339143-7

25 26 27 28 29 PCA 10 9 8 7 6 5 4 3 2 1

To my children, Charlie and Claire

May you never lose the sparkle and joy of celebrating every day and holidays. You are cuter than a bug's ear! I love you with all my heart.

love,
TM, "the Mama"

INTRODUCTION

As a wife and mama of two who loves celebrating seasons and holidays, I know firsthand not only that time is the best gift you can give someone but also how quickly it flies by—in a blink! The days are long, but the years are short. My love language for my family is making fun recipes and adding a touch of festivity to meals, whether for an ordinary day or a special occasion. It fills my heart with happiness and builds a connection with my children on a whole different level of fun. These memories bring me comfort and warmth, reminding me of a life well lived.

Did you know that our sense of smell and taste are strongly connected to childhood memories and nostalgia? They have incredible power to evoke vivid recollections and emotions from the past. Like, have you ever smelled a candle that took you straight back to a certain time of your life?

You will never regret going the extra mile to create joyful family memories.

Creating happy family memories can be both simple and imperfect. It doesn't matter how much you have or the size of your home. What your family will remember most is how you made them feel. You will never regret going the extra mile to create joyful family memories. And a little daily celebrating is actually pretty easy—you can start anytime, exactly where you are right now.

For me, it all began with a holiday tradition with my mom. We would make an Easter bunny cake every year. You know the one! We'd add coconut for fur, licorice for whiskers, and jelly beans for the eyes. I looked forward to making that cake every Easter, but little did I know that this sweet family memory would one day direct my professional life at my blog *Best Friends for Frosting*, leading me to help others celebrate their families and loved ones by making new food memories of their own. When I started *Best Friends for Frosting* in 2011, I began sharing my recipes and party ideas to celebrate the everyday, every day. And, not surprisingly, to this day, we still go all out for all the holidays and seasons.

Although I held my own favorite childhood food memories in my heart, it wasn't until I became a mom that my passion for creating happy family food memories came full circle. The journey to discovering this passion, however, wasn't easy. When I was twenty-three, my husband, Andy, and I found out I was pregnant, and while my friends were busy navigating their college years and starting their careers, I embraced my new identity as a first-time mom. Dealing with the whirlwind of motherhood was tough on its own, but when postpartum depression and anxiety hit, it felt like I was stuck in a foggy maze of worries and heaviness. Not only did I feel disconnected from motherhood, but I judged myself and thought I was a terrible person for feeling this way. I honestly never in a million years thought I would ever talk about postpartum depression in a book, let alone discuss it at the dinner table.

That blazing summer in 2010, shortly after I gave birth, must have been the longest one of my life. But as the heat gave way to the crispness of fall, I took baby Charlie to the pumpkin patch, a place I hadn't been to since I was a little girl, and I couldn't help but feel deeply connected to the experience through Charlie's eyes. It brought back happy, nostalgic memories, reminding me of the joyous moments of my own childhood. The experience opened up a vault, and I was overwhelmed with memories of seasonal and holiday activities from my past, each bringing back joy and excitement, through which I started to connect with motherhood. The warm and inviting freshly baked hot apple cider donuts, the familiar scent and texture of the hay on the hayride, and the way the pumpkins glowed under the sun's golden rays filled my senses. I truly never wanted that fall season to end.

And when I tell you I didn't want it to end, I'm not kidding. Our family would stretch out holidays and seasons for as long as possible because it was our happy place. I loved how connected to my family I felt, from the joy of scoring a cute new holiday decoration from HomeGoods to the excitement of trying new recipes to the comfort of seasonal candles. I discovered this was my love language, finding joy and purpose in these moments.

I wholeheartedly believe everything happens for a reason, and perhaps my struggles were meant to lead me down this challenging path so that I could help other moms strengthen their family connections by encouraging them to choose positivity, embrace loved ones, and create lasting family food memories by celebrating everyday moments, holidays, and seasons.

Create lasting family food memories by celebrating everyday moments, holidays, and seasons.

Whether you're on a budget, short on time, or both, I've got you covered with joyous food. Create extraordinary meals without breaking the bank. Try my tried-and-true recipes, like my internet-famous Million-Dollar Spaghetti (page 22), our family-favorite Taco Soup (page 49), my mother-in-law's crowd-pleasing Rustic Tortellini Soup (page 28), and more! Get year-round inspiration with the "Holiday Cheer All Year" chapter, featuring fun family treats like Pretzel Shamrocks (page 183), Bunny Cinnamon Rolls (page 184), Graveyard Pudding Cups (page 198), and Oreo Cookie Santas (page 210). You'll find festive icons sprinkled throughout, bookmarking recipes perfect for your holiday celebrations! And I help

There is no better time than now to sprinkle happiness within your own four walls at home.

simplify your holiday planning with practical tips and strategies for creating lasting memories, bringing loved ones together, starting family traditions, and making the ordinary extraordinary.

Join me on this journey of celebration and memory-making. Let's create joyful and nostalgic family food memories that will be treasured for years. It's not about perfection but about the love and joy you bring to your family through the meals you prepare.

There is no better time than now to sprinkle happiness within your own four walls at home. The grass is not greener on the other side; it is greenest where you water it most. I am so excited to share these super-easy recipes that I hope will one day become happy, nostalgic memories for your family, too. If I could bear-hug you through this book, I totally would! Here's to building your very own legacy of joyful family food memories. Celebrate every day and make every moment count.

Love, Melissa

EASY BREAKFASTS

Rise and shine! Every day is a brand-new opportunity to kick off the morning with a fresh start as strong as your cup of coffee. (Unless you're like me—I thought I liked coffee, but it turns out I just like creamer!) Breakfast is one of the best things you can do to care for yourself and your family. It fuels your body with energy after fasting during sleep, preventing that midmorning crash and helping you feel energized. It gives us that extra pep in our step, and sets the tone for a happy and productive day.

This chapter includes some of my favorite easy breakfast go-tos that simplify my morning routine. Whether you're short on time and need an easy make-ahead recipe, planning meals for the week, or hosting a breakfast gathering for a group, I've got you covered. Many of these recipes can be lovingly prepared in batches, making starting your day on a happy note even easier. From convenient halfway-homemade shortcuts to muffin-tin hacks, these recipes are designed to make your mornings more manageable, enjoyable, and stress-free. Just think of breakfast as a mini celebration for the day ahead. You've got this!

Sausage, Egg, *and* Cheese Breakfast Roll-Ups

Makes 16 roll-ups

6 large eggs

1 tablespoon milk

¼ teaspoon salt

1 teaspoon olive oil

Two 8-ounce cans Pillsbury Crescent Rolls

8 slices American cheese

16 breakfast sausage links, cooked

Maple syrup, for serving

Whether you're rushing out the door to school, heading to a baseball game, or feeding a house full of hungry kids after an epic sleepover, these roll-ups are a convenient, quick, and easy grab-and-go recipe. You need only a few well-loved classic breakfast ingredients to whip up this satisfying breakfast quickly for those busy mornings. The combination of flaky crescent rolls, fluffy eggs, melty cheese, and savory sausage is irresistible. And if sausage isn't your thing, you can easily switch it up with fully cooked bacon. These are always such a hit with our family!

1. Preheat the oven to 350°F. Line a baking sheet with parchment paper.

2. In a medium bowl, beat the eggs, milk, and salt together until combined.

3. In a large nonstick skillet, heat the oil over medium heat. Add the eggs and scramble until cooked, about 5 minutes.

4. Unroll the crescent roll dough and separate it into triangles. Cut the cheese slices in half and place one half on each crescent roll. Top with scrambled eggs and one cooked sausage link. Roll up each crescent roll and place it on the lined baking sheet.

5. Bake for about 15 minutes, or until the crescents are golden brown.

6. Serve immediately with maple syrup for dipping.

STORAGE

Place fully cooled roll-ups in an airtight container and refrigerate for up to 3 days. Reheat individual roll-ups in the microwave for about 40 seconds.

Sausage Hash Brown Cups

I'm a sucker for any recipe that uses a muffin tin in unexpected ways! These Sausage Hash Brown Cups will bring joy to your breakfast table. Just pop your muffin tin in the oven and watch while everyone wakes up to the joy of smelling homemade breakfast. These easy breakfast cups are always a hit with my husband, Andy, and the kids. The combination of cheesy hash browns and savory sausage is a match made in heaven. They're perfect for a weekday breakfast or a special holiday brunch. And did I mention they are grab-and-go?

Makes 12 cups

1. Preheat the oven to 400°F. Grease 12 cups of a muffin tin with cooking spray.

2. In a large skillet, cook the breakfast sausage over medium-high heat, breaking up the sausage as you cook, until the meat is no longer pink and is golden brown, about 12 minutes.

3. In a large bowl, beat the eggs with the milk until combined. Add the sausage, bell pepper, onion, bacon, and half of the cheddar to the egg mixture and mix until combined.

4. Add 3 or 4 Tater Tots to each muffin cup. Fill each cup three-quarters full with the egg mixture and sprinkle with the remaining cheese.

5. Bake until the eggs are set, 15 to 20 minutes.

6. Garnish with the chives and serve immediately.

Cooking spray

1 pound loose breakfast sausage meat

6 large eggs

1 tablespoon milk

¼ cup diced red bell pepper

½ cup diced onion

¼ cup store-bought real bacon bits or chopped cooked bacon

3 cups shredded cheddar cheese

3 cups frozen Ore-Ida Tater Tots, thawed

Chopped fresh chives, for serving

Ham, Egg, *and* Cheese Cups

If there is ONE recipe you will make from this chapter, pick these Ham, Egg, and Cheese Cups! I love making these because they're healthy, they taste incredible, and you can even batch the egg cups in a muffin pan! These are an absolute game changer in our house, and I often make them every week. With just a few ingredients and in less than 30 minutes, you'll have a protein-packed, low-carb breakfast that will make you feel like a superstar. Pop them in the oven, let them cool, and enjoy an outstanding grab-and-go breakfast that will set your day up for success with a smile!

Makes 12 cups

Cooking spray

12 slices ham

2 cups shredded cheddar cheese

12 large eggs

Kosher salt and freshly ground black pepper

Chopped fresh chives, for serving

1. Preheat the oven to 400°F.

2. Grease 12 cups of a muffin tin with cooking spray and line each cup with a slice of the ham. If the ham doesn't fit, trim it with a knife.

3. Divide the cheddar evenly among the cups, crack an egg into each cup, and season with salt and pepper to taste.

4. Bake until the eggs are set, 16 to 18 minutes.

5. Remove the egg cups from the muffin tin with a spoon, garnish with the chives, and serve.

Mini Banana Pancakes

Serves 4

Mini Banana Pancakes are a reader and family favorite at *Best Friends for Frosting* that everyone goes wild over! Imagine biting into a fluffy pancake with a sweet banana surprise inside. They're fruity and light, making them a perfect afternoon snack. Serve plain, with syrup, or even with a drizzle of chocolate or peanut butter on top. It's like a burst of happiness in every bite.

3 cups your favorite pancake mix (I like Krusteaz)

1 tablespoon vegetable oil

4 bananas

FOR SERVING (optional)

Peanut butter

Mini chocolate chips

Maple syrup

1. Prepare the pancake batter according to the package directions.

2. Heat a large skillet over medium heat and add the vegetable oil.

3. Slice the bananas into ¾-inch-thick coins, dip each slice into the batter, and add to the skillet. Cook until golden brown, about 1 minute per side.

4. To serve: If desired, drizzle with warmed peanut butter, mini chocolate chips, and/or maple syrup.

CELEBRATING TIP

Make breakfast a party by bringing out a muffin tin filled with various toppings, such as sprinkles or chopped peanuts. Whether you're customizing for the everyday or a special occasion, serve these in festive muffin liners with patterns like polka dots, gingham, and stripes.

Spinach *and* Bacon Quiche

My mom, Mama Nancy, has been making her family-famous Spinach and Bacon Quiche for as long as I can remember. I instantly associate the smell and flavor of this quiche with some of my life's most joyous occasions and milestones, like my garden baby shower with Claire, bringing both kids home from the hospital, and cozy Christmas mornings. But Mama Nancy didn't just make it to celebrate special days. She would easily whip it up on lazy weekends using premade refrigerated pie crust and a few ingredients. Other times, she would surprise us with it just because she wanted to add extra joy to our day! That's what I call celebrating every day!

Serves 8

4 large eggs

2 cups half-and-half

⅛ teaspoon ground nutmeg

1 sheet refrigerated pie dough

1 tablespoon salted butter, melted

One 10-ounce bag frozen spinach, thawed and drained

½ cup store-bought real bacon bits or chopped cooked bacon

4 ounces Swiss cheese, shredded

1. Preheat the oven to 425°F.

2. In a medium bowl, beat together the eggs, half-and-half, and nutmeg until combined.

3. Unroll the pie dough, brush both sides with the melted butter, and use the dough to line a 9-inch pie pan. Trim the edges and crimp.

4. Evenly sprinkle the spinach, bacon, and Swiss cheese over the pie crust. Pour in the egg mixture.

5. Bake uncovered for 15 minutes. Reduce the oven temperature to 350°F and bake for 30 minutes more, or until a knife inserted in the center comes out clean.

6. Let stand for 5 minutes before slicing and serving.

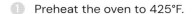

CELEBRATING TIP

Invest in future nostalgic family memories by finding one recipe your family loves that you can whip up a few times a year to make every day feel like a special occasion. Bonus: Preschedule three dates on your calendar to make it throughout the year.

STORAGE

Wrap each quiche slice individually in foil and keep in the refrigerator for up to 3 days. To reheat, place foil-wrapped slices in a 325°F oven for 15 to 20 minutes, until heated through.

Breakfast Sliders

Serves 6

12 large eggs

¼ cup milk

½ teaspoon salt

1 teaspoon olive oil

12 slices bacon

12 Hawaiian rolls (not pulled apart)

3 tablespoons salted butter, melted

12 slices cheddar cheese

Last year, we kicked off a new family tradition with a trip to Sunriver, Oregon. If you haven't visited before, I'd 10/10 recommend it! We gathered with our extended family at our wonderful friends Justin and Jessica's cozy condo resort, surrounded by forests and gorgeous scenery. We went fishing—Charlie caught a rainbow trout!—and took a shuttle to the top of Lava Butte, a five-thousand-foot volcano, and even went river tubing for the first time! We had the best time!

We didn't eat out once during that trip, and all took turns making meals. When it was my turn to whip up breakfast, I knew exactly what I was going to make: my never-fail Breakfast Sliders. Not only are these sliders easy to assemble and make ahead, but they're always a hit! Even my picky-eater nephew, Toby, enjoys them!

Inspired by our love for Hawaiian rolls, I created these sliders using our favorite breakfast ingredients—eggs, bacon, and cheese. Layered on soft and fluffy rolls, it's a combination made in breakfast heaven! And to add that extra touch of flavor, I brush the tops with melted butter for a golden and irresistible finish.

Whether it's a special holiday brunch, a fun weekend treat, or just because I want to celebrate every day, these sliders always hit the spot.

1. Preheat the oven to 350°F.

2. In a large bowl, beat together the eggs, milk, and salt until combined.

3. In a large nonstick skillet, heat the oil over medium heat. Add the eggs and scramble for about 3 minutes, or until cooked to your liking.

4. In a separate skillet, cook the bacon over medium heat until crispy, about 5 minutes per side. Transfer the cooked bacon to a paper towel–lined plate to drain.

5. Cut the sheet of Hawaiian rolls in half horizontally, keeping the tops of the rolls and the bottoms of the rolls together (like a giant slider).

6. Place the bottom half of the rolls on a baking sheet, cut side up. Brush half of the melted butter over the rolls. Layer on the bacon, scrambled eggs, and cheddar, then add the top half of the rolls, closing the giant slider. Brush the tops of the rolls with the remaining melted butter.

7. Bake until the cheese is melted and the rolls are lightly browned, about 15 minutes.

8. Let cool for 5 minutes before slicing and serving.

Muffin Tin "Pancakes"

Makes 12 "pancakes"

Prepare for the cuteness overload of these mini muffin pancakes! They are so simple to make—just pour in your favorite prepared pancake batter, add your favorite toppings, and bake away. You can even store them in the freezer so they're readily available to grab quickly on busy mornings. They're also perfect for when hosting a sleepover and feeding a house full of giggly pigtailed girlies in pajamas. They're worth every bite!

Cooking spray

3½ cups your favorite pancake mix (I like Krusteaz)

3 tablespoons blueberries (optional)

3 tablespoons chocolate chips (optional)

3 tablespoons sprinkles (optional)

Maple syrup, for serving

1. Preheat the oven to 350°F. Grease 12 cups of a muffin tin with cooking spray.

2. In a medium bowl, mix together the pancake mix with 2⅓ cups water until combined. Fill each muffin cup half to three-quarters full of batter. Add some of each of the toppings, if using, to each muffin cup.

3. Bake the "pancakes" for about 15 minutes, or until a toothpick inserted into the center comes out clean.

4. Serve immediately, with maple syrup.

STORAGE

Store completely cooled pancake muffins in an airtight container for up to 4 days in the refrigerator or up to 3 months in the freezer. To thaw, place frozen muffins in the refrigerator overnight or on the counter for a couple of hours.

CELEBRATING TIP

Customize your Muffin Tin "Pancakes" to your heart's content with topping options to make it feel like a celebration. Are you a candy lover? Add M&M's or Reese's Pieces. Feeling fruity? Add some fresh bananas, strawberries, or raspberries. Does someone have a birthday? Use colorful sprinkles like confetti for a birthday breakfast treat! Is it the month of your favorite holiday? Get creative with seasonal colored sprinkles for all the holidays.

add a little

YAY

to every day

Sheet Pan Pancakes

Long gone are the days when you make four pancakes at a time in the same pan. Sheet Pan Pancakes are one of the easiest breakfast recipes for serving a crowd. Bake large batches in the oven and serve hot to everyone simultaneously. All you have to do is line a baking sheet with parchment paper, add pancake mix, and top with your favorite toppings—from sprinkles to fruit to nuts to chocolate chips to just plain Jane. There are so many fun ways to customize these and sprinkle extra joy.

If you make and freeze these ahead, just thaw them for an hour before reheating them for the kids. The excitement of pancakes for breakfast will distract from the rushed hustle and bustle.

Makes 12 square pancakes

3 cups your favorite pancake mix (I like Krusteaz)

2 cups sliced strawberries

1 cup blueberries

Maple syrup, for serving

1. Preheat the oven to 425°F. Line a 13 × 18–inch baking sheet with parchment paper.

2. In a large bowl, mix the pancake mix with 2 cups water until just combined. (Alternatively, prepare the pancake batter according to the package directions.)

3. Pour the batter onto the lined baking sheet and even it out with the back of a spoon. Top the batter with the sliced strawberries and blueberries.

4. Bake for about 15 minutes, or until the pancake is golden brown.

5. Cut the pancake into 12 squares and serve immediately with maple syrup.

STORAGE

Store completely cooled Sheet Pan Pancakes in an airtight container for up to 4 days in the refrigerator or up to 3 months in the freezer. To thaw, place the pancake squares in the refrigerator overnight or on the counter for an hour.

Custard Toast

Picture this: crunchy edges of toast, a soft and custardy center, and a creamy, cheesecake-like filling. Custard Toast is almost like French toast's and cheese Danish's long-lost cousin. It's like eating cake for breakfast but without the guilt, because this recipe uses Greek yogurt instead of cream. Trust me, once you try it, you'll be hooked, too!

Serves 2

1 large egg

3 tablespoons full-fat vanilla Greek yogurt

1 tablespoon maple syrup, plus more for serving

2 thick slices soft bread or Texas toast

5 raspberries

2 tablespoons chocolate chips

1. Preheat the oven to 350°F. Line a baking sheet with parchment paper.

2. In a small bowl, whisk together the egg, yogurt, and maple syrup to form the custard.

3. Place the slices of bread on the lined baking sheet. With your fingers, press into the middle of each slice (without tearing it) to create a well for the custard. Using a spoon, fill the centers with custard mix. Top each with raspberries and chocolate chips.

4. Bake for 15 to 20 minutes, until the custard sets.

5. Let cool for 5 minutes before serving. Drizzle with maple syrup.

FAMILY-FRIENDLY DINNERS

Dinnertime doesn't have to be a struggle! If the daily "What's for dinner?" question leaves you feeling stressed, this chapter is for you. I've compiled seventeen of our favorite tried-and-true family dinner recipes, many inspired by my Italian roots—think Million-Dollar Spaghetti (page 22), Lazy Ravioli Lasagna (page 27), and more! These easy family-friendly dinner recipes are simple, delicious, and perfect for busy weeknights. Get ready for meals that you can assemble in minutes, leaving you more time for the good stuff—making memories at the dinner table!

Imagine starting your Sunday morning with a warm cup of coffee, your favorite song playing, and zero interruptions. This is your Sunday reset. You pick out five easy recipes from your master list that can be assembled with just a few ingredients. You quickly add the ingredients to your online shopping cart and schedule a grocery order. Your new meal planner is already printed (see page 20), so all you need to do is write down with your favorite pen—*a pink gel pen for me, please!*—the meals you plan to make and stick the plan on the refrigerator. You set an alarm to start dinner at 4:30 p.m. so it will be on the table by 5:15 p.m.

See how smoothly the week has flown by? Your meal plan is your passport to an entire week of easy dinners, leaving more room to say YES to happy moments with those who matter most!

MEAL PLANNING

made easy

The key to successful meal planning is finding recipes that are easy to prepare, require minimal ingredients, and are enjoyed by the whole family. With a little time and effort, you can create a meal-planning routine that truly works. On the opposite page are some of my tips to help make meal planning easier. Create a master list of your favorite doable recipes or choose from this chapter's family-friendly dinner recipes. This will save you hours of meal-planning time and decision fatigue.

*Say goodbye to "What's for dinner?" and hello to organized meal planning with my FREE printable meal planner. Available at **BestFriendsForFrosting.com/FreePrintables.***

Establish a regular meal-planning routine. Set aside a specific time each week to plan, such as Sunday morning or Saturday afternoon. It takes 21 days to form a habit and 90 days to make it a permanent lifestyle change. The secret to getting ahead is just getting started.

Check your pantry, fridge, and freezer before shopping to utilize ingredients you already have.

Commit to making three recipes each week to avoid overload. Balance out your meal plan with simple staples like chicken nuggets or quesadillas when you need a break. Remember, we're choosing purpose over perfection!

Display your meal plan where it is easily visible. Tape it to the refrigerator for everyone to see.

⑤

Grocery delivery and pickup services will be your best friends—besides me! They will save you so much time.

Plan to take a break from cooking one day each week. Order takeout or have a designated "easy meal" day. When I was growing up, my parents got either Chinese food or pizza and rented a movie every Friday. I came across an online meme that said, "I used to think my parents did pizza and a movie on Friday nights to be fun, but now I know they were just tired!" LOL, it's so true!

⑦

Buy quick and easy sides, such as bagged salad kits or vegetables ready for roasting.

Have backup options for lazy nights, such as keeping frozen breaded chicken patties or fish sticks on hand.

Remember, done is better than perfect. Don't strive for perfection, just get dinner on the table.

happy meal planning!

Million-Dollar Spaghetti

Serves 8

Kosher salt

16 ounces spaghetti pasta

1 pound loose Italian sausage

Two 24-ounce jars marinara sauce

One 32-ounce container ricotta cheese

8 ounces shredded mozzarella cheese

Chopped fresh parsley, for serving

I'll never forget the day I hit "publish" on my Million-Dollar Spaghetti recipe on TikTok. In all my years sharing recipes on the internet, I've never had a recipe go so viral. I was at the park with the kids, lying in the sunshine on a red gingham picnic blanket, and my phone was blowing up with hundreds of thousands of notifications. I got so distracted that I didn't realize until too late that the kids had pulled out a massive chunk of grass from the otherwise neatly manicured lawn. Out of the corner of my eye, I saw that they had neatly piled the grass they'd pulled. That explained their unusually good behavior while I wasn't paying attention. I had to remind myself the grass is the greenest where I water it most.

Our family LOVES this million-dollar baked spaghetti recipe. My husband, Andy, prefers it over lasagna any day . . . and let me tell you, I make good lasagna, too! This spaghetti is one of the easiest yet most flavorful dinner recipes to include in your meal-planning rotation. All you have to do is add layers of marinara sauce, spaghetti pasta, ricotta cheese, more spaghetti pasta, cooked Italian sausage, and marinara sauce again, then sprinkle mozzarella cheese on top. Bake, garnish with parsley, and dinner is served!

1. Preheat the oven to 350°F.

2. Bring a pot of salted water to a boil over high heat. Just think of the ocean—your water should be salty like the sea. Add the spaghetti and cook according to the package directions, until al dente. Drain the spaghetti and set aside.

3. Meanwhile, heat a large skillet over medium-high heat. Add the Italian sausage and cook, breaking up the sausage as you cook, until the meat is no longer pink and is golden brown, about 12 minutes. Drain off the excess fat and set aside.

recipe continues

4   Pour a jar of the marinara sauce into a 9 × 13–inch baking dish. Add half of the cooked spaghetti and all of the ricotta cheese. Top with the remaining spaghetti, the cooked sausage, the remaining jar of marinara sauce, and the mozzarella cheese on top.

5   Bake uncovered until the mozzarella is browned and bubbling, 35 to 40 minutes.

6   Let cool for 10 minutes before serving. Garnish with parsley.

BE SOMEBODY WHO
MAKES EVERYBODY
FEEL LIKE
somebody

Lazy Ravioli Lasagna

As an Italian American, I often joke that this easy three-ingredient lazy lasagna is the long-lost cousin of traditional lasagna. Not only does this make-ahead recipe deliver the same delicious flavors, but it's also one of the quickest halfway-homemade shortcuts out there. All you do is layer ravioli, marinara sauce, and mozzarella cheese and bake away! Alternatively, you could use Alfredo sauce instead of spaghetti sauce for a richer flavor. Give it a try and enjoy the versatility of this easy and flavorful dish! Always remember, done is better than perfect! Time-saving shortcuts will allow you to quickly put a family meal on the table while having more quality time with your loved ones.

Serves 8

Two 24-ounce jars marinara sauce

One 48-ounce bag frozen cheese ravioli

4 cups shredded mozzarella cheese

Chopped fresh parsley, for serving

1. Preheat the oven to 400°F.

2. Pour half a jar of marinara sauce into a 9 × 13-inch baking dish and spread into an even layer. Layer in half of the ravioli, another half jar of marinara sauce, and 2 cups of the mozzarella. Add the remaining ravioli, the entire second jar of marinara sauce, and the remaining 2 cups mozzarella.

3. Bake uncovered until cooked through and the mozzarella is melted, 30 to 40 minutes.

4. Let cool for 10 minutes before serving. Garnish with chopped parsley.

QUICK TIP

Pair lazy lasagna with salad and garlic bread by picking up ready-made garlic bread from the grocery store bakery and grabbing a Caesar salad kit. Need extra protein? Grab a rotisserie chicken and bulk up your salad. It's a brilliant combination for a hassle-free meal.

Rustic Tortellini Soup

Serves 6

1 pound loose Italian sausage

1 large onion, chopped

4 garlic cloves, minced

1 teaspoon Italian seasoning

Two 14.5-ounce cans chicken broth

One 14.5-ounce can diced tomatoes, undrained

One 9-ounce package refrigerated cheese tortellini

One 6-ounce package fresh baby spinach, chopped

¾ teaspoon dried basil

Shredded parmesan cheese, for serving

Chopped fresh basil, for serving

Whenever my mother-in-law, Barbara, makes her Rustic Tortellini Soup, everyone who tries it wants the recipe. It's that good! My soup-enthusiast son, Charlie, ranks it among his top favorite soups, and it's become one of my go-to soup recipes. It's quick to prepare on a busy night and packed with healthy, flavorful ingredients. I always make a double batch so there are leftovers for the next day. Add spicy links, turkey sausage, or ground turkey for an extra kick and even more protein. When you cook this soup, your house will be filled with the comforting aromas of an Italian restaurant!

1. In a large Dutch oven or pot, cook the sausage and onion over medium-high heat, breaking up the sausage as you cook, until the meat is no longer pink and is golden brown, about 12 minutes.

2. Add the garlic and Italian seasoning and cook for an additional 2 minutes. Stir in the broth, 1¾ cups water, and diced tomatoes with their juices. Bring to a boil over high heat. Add the tortellini and cook for 8 minutes.

3. Reduce the heat to low and fold in the spinach. Add the dried basil and cook for an additional 2 minutes.

4. Serve with shredded parmesan cheese and chopped fresh basil.

STORAGE

If you double this soup recipe to have leftovers, cook the tortellini separately and store them in their own airtight container. This will prevent them from getting mushy.

MAKE THE ORDINARY
Extraordinary

No-Boil Pasta Bake

Can you tell I love Italian recipes?! This one-pan pasta bake will make you feel like a total magician, as boiling the pasta is not required—just pop it in the oven and watch the pasta cook perfectly. Cooking pasta right in the sauce saves time and cuts down on dishes. My husband, Andy, and I both love making this easy dinner recipe. Whether you're a beginner cook or teaching your child to cook, this recipe will make you feel like a kitchen rock star! With only 5 minutes of prep time, it's a miracle recipe for those busy weeknights.

Serves 8

16 ounces penne pasta

One 2-pound bag frozen fully cooked meatballs

Two 24-ounce jars marinara sauce

3 cups shredded mozzarella cheese

Chopped fresh basil, for serving

1. Preheat the oven to 425°F.

2. In a 9 × 13-inch baking dish, combine the pasta, meatballs, marinara sauce, and 2 cups water and mix until evenly combined. Cover with foil.

3. Bake for 1 hour.

4. Remove from the oven. Uncover, top with the mozzarella, and return it to the oven to bake uncovered until the cheese is bubbling and melted, about 15 minutes.

5. Let cool for 10 minutes before topping with chopped basil. Serve.

Marry Me Chicken

This is my take on the viral recipe trend that originated with Lindsay Funston at Delish. I promise you'll fall head over heels for the irresistible taste of Marry Me Chicken—I turn to this recipe whenever I'm planning a romantic dinner, want to indulge in an extra-special weeknight treat, or need to butter up my husband, Andy, before asking a huge favor! It works every time! I start by searing chicken breasts to golden, moist perfection, then I smother them in a creamy, satisfying sauce that is flavorful in every bite. Serve this dish with French bread to soak up the creamy juices and a tangy green salad to balance the flavors. Don't be afraid to double the recipe; the leftovers reheat well and make a fantastic lunch the next day.

Serves 2 generously

2 large boneless, skinless chicken breasts

Kosher salt

¼ cup all-purpose flour

¼ cup olive oil

3 tablespoons unsalted butter

4 garlic cloves, minced

1 tablespoon tomato paste

½ teaspoon Italian seasoning

1 cup low-sodium chicken broth

¾ cup heavy cream

½ cup grated parmesan cheese, plus more for serving

½ cup sliced oil-packed sun-dried tomatoes

Shredded fresh basil leaves, for garnish

1. Starting with the thickest part of each chicken breast, slice in half horizontally to create a total of 4 cutlets. Season with salt, pound each cutlet with a mallet to tenderize, then lightly coat each side of the cutlets with the flour.

2. In a large skillet, heat the oil over medium heat and add the butter. Once the butter is melted, working in batches to not crowd the pan, add the chicken cutlets and cook until golden brown, about 4 minutes per side. Remove the cutlets from the pan and set aside.

3. Reduce the heat under the skillet to low, add the garlic, and cook until fragrant, 1 to 2 minutes. Add the tomato paste, Italian seasoning, and chicken broth and stir to combine. Increase the heat to medium and bring to a simmer. Deglaze, scraping any browned bits from the bottom of the pan, and cook until the liquid is reduced by half, about 5 minutes.

4. Stir in the heavy cream and cook for 3 to 4 minutes to thicken the sauce. Stir in the parmesan and sun-dried tomatoes and season the sauce with salt to taste. Add the chicken cutlets and cook for an additional 5 minutes.

5. Serve garnished with fresh basil and more grated parmesan.

Hawaiian Pizza Pasta Bake

Serves 8

Kosher salt

16 ounces penne pasta

Two 24-ounce jars marinara sauce

2 cups diced ham

One 20-ounce can diced pineapple, drained

1 medium onion, diced

⅔ cup store-bought real bacon bits or crumbled cooked bacon

3 cups shredded mozzarella cheese

Chopped green onions, for serving

This Hawaiian Pizza Pasta Bake holds such a special place in my heart—it was the first dinner recipe I ever made with my daughter, Claire, when she was just four years old. Taking classic dishes and putting a unique spin on the recipe makes dinner around the table that much more memorable. We love Italian food and Hawaiian pizza, so you can only imagine my excitement when I found a way to combine the best of both worlds in one dish! If you're not a Hawaiian pizza fan, swap the ham and pineapple for pepperoni.

1. Preheat the oven to 350°F.

2. Bring a large pot of salted water to a boil over high heat. Just think of the ocean—your water should be salty like the sea. Add the pasta and cook according to the package directions, until al dente. Drain the pasta and place in a large bowl.

3. Add the marinara sauce, 1½ cups of the ham, three-quarters of the diced pineapple, onion, and bacon to the pasta and toss to combine.

4. Spoon the pasta mixture into a 9 × 13-inch baking dish and top with the mozzarella and the remaining pineapple and ham.

5. Bake uncovered until the edges are golden brown, about 1 hour.

6. Let cool for 10 minutes before serving sprinkled with green onions.

Taco Pizza Roll-Ups

I feel like I am always craving either tacos or pizza. But when I crave tacos AND pizza? These taco pizza rolls are the answer! They're made with flavorful taco meat and gooey cheese, all rolled up in pizza dough—it's pure deliciousness. Ready in under 30 minutes, the rolls are baked to perfection and served with sour cream and salsa. Snack time? Dinnertime? Party time? It's always the right time to celebrate every day with this tasty treat!

Makes 8 roll-ups

1. Preheat the oven to 400°F. Line a baking sheet with parchment paper.

2. In a large skillet, cook the ground beef over medium heat until cooked through, 8 to 10 minutes.

3. Add the taco seasoning and ⅔ cup water and bring to a boil. Reduce the heat to medium and simmer for 2 minutes.

4. Unroll the pizza dough and use a rolling pin to roll it into an even ¼-inch-thick sheet. Place the dough on a cutting board. Distribute the taco meat and cheese evenly over the dough. Place in the refrigerator or freezer for 10 to 15 minutes to firm up the dough.

5. Starting from a long side, roll up the dough tightly into a log. Cut the roll crosswise into eight 1-inch-thick pieces. Place the rolls on the lined baking sheet.

6. Bake until the crust is golden brown, about 12 minutes.

7. Serve topped with sour cream, salsa, and green onions.

1 pound ground beef

One 1-ounce packet taco seasoning

One 13.8-ounce can refrigerated pizza dough

2½ cups Mexican blend shredded cheese

FOR SERVING

Sour cream

Salsa

Chopped green onions

Mini Chicken Pot Pies

Serves 6

Cooking spray

2 cups chopped cooked chicken breast

One 10.5-ounce can low-sodium condensed cream of chicken soup

½ cup store-bought real bacon bits or chopped cooked bacon

One 10-ounce bag frozen mixed vegetables

12 refrigerated biscuits (I like Pillsbury)

Part of celebrating every day means trying well-loved recipes in new ways to make every day feel special! My son, Mr. Charlie, is the official chicken-pot-pie lover in our house. As cooking is one of my love languages, I excitedly put together this five-ingredient make-ahead recipe using a muffin tin—because muffin tins are not only for sweet desserts. They are one of the best shortcuts for mini foods.

1. Preheat the oven to 350°F. Grease 12 cups of a muffin tin with cooking spray.

2. In a large bowl, mix together the chicken breast, cream of chicken soup, bacon, and mixed vegetables.

3. Place a biscuit in each cup of the muffin tin and use a shot glass or tablespoon to press down in the centers to create pockets for the filling. Fill each biscuit with the chicken/vegetable mixture.

4. Bake for 30 to 35 minutes, until the biscuits are golden brown.

5. Let cool on a wire rack for 5 minutes before serving.

STORAGE

Store any leftover cooked veggies and sausage
in an airtight container in the refrigerator for
up to 3 days. To reheat, preheat the oven to
350°F. Spread leftovers on a baking sheet and
heat for 10 to 15 minutes, or until hot.

Vegetable Sausage Roast

My parents habitually buy things in bulk at Costco and give us what they don't like or no longer need. My dad went through a quick keto phase and gave us some sausage. My husband, Andy, was thinking of a creative way to use it for dinner, and that led to one of our favorite healthful family dinners that you can make all on one baking sheet. Andy has now made this Vegetable Sausage Roast for years, and it's a massive hit with our family of four. And here's the best part—minimal dishes! Just chop everything on a cutting board, add it to a baking sheet, and roast away! Serve this with store-bought dipping sauces, make your own, or enjoy it plain. We often make extra, as it reheats well for a quick lunch the following day. It's like getting a bonus meal without any additional effort.

Serves 4

1. Preheat the oven to 425°F.

2. In a large bowl, combine the potatoes, sweet potatoes, Brussels sprouts, bell peppers, onion, and oil and toss until evenly coated. Spread the vegetables into an even layer on a baking sheet and sprinkle with salt to taste and add the garlic powder.

3. Bake the vegetables for 15 minutes.

4. Remove the baking sheet from the oven and evenly arrange the sausage slices over the vegetables. Return to the oven and bake for an additional 15 minutes, until the sausage pieces are browned.

5. Serve immediately garnished with parsley.

3 large potatoes, peeled and cut into 1-inch cubes

3 large sweet potatoes, peeled and cut into 1-inch cubes

1 pound Brussels sprouts, trimmed and halved

1 red bell pepper, thinly sliced

1 yellow bell pepper, thinly sliced

1 medium red onion, thinly sliced

2 tablespoons extra virgin olive oil

Kosher salt

2 teaspoons garlic powder

One 14-ounce fully cooked Polish sausage, cut into 1-inch pieces

Chopped fresh parsley, for serving

Lasagna Zucchini Boats

Serves 8

8 large zucchini

1 pound loose Italian sausage

2 cups jarred marinara sauce

2 cups ricotta cheese

2 cups shredded mozzarella cheese

Chopped fresh parsley, for serving

I should have called this the lasagna spin-off chapter. There are so many fun ways to incorporate marinara sauce; this is one of my favorite healthy ways to include it. Rest assured, if you're a lasagna fan, I will bet money you'll love these zucchini boats. Even my kids, Charlie and Claire, enjoy this. Talk about being kid-friendly! And because you get your meat and vegetables in one dish, making it for dinner makes me feel like a super mom!

This lasagna alternative is a fun and healthy way to incorporate more vegetables into meals, especially during the summer, when zucchini is in season.

1. Preheat the oven to 350°F.

2. Halve each zucchini lengthwise, then score and scoop out the seeds. Slice a thin layer off the bottom of the zucchini halves so they will sit flat. Arrange them, scooped side up, on a large baking sheet.

3. In a large skillet, cook the Italian sausage over medium-high heat, breaking up the sausage as you cook, until the meat is no longer pink and the sausage is cooked through, about 12 minutes. Add the marinara sauce and stir to combine. Remove from the heat.

4. Divide the ricotta among the zucchini halves and spread evenly in the bottom of each. Spoon the sausage mixture over the ricotta layer and evenly sprinkle with the mozzarella.

5. Bake until the zucchini is tender and the cheese is melted, about 30 minutes.

6. Serve garnished with parsley.

Taco Soup

There's a saying: "A few people will change your life forever. Find them!" That happened for me when I met one of my closest friends, MaryAnn, through Instagram. As I was meal planning for the week, she insisted that I try her family's go-to favorite taco soup recipe. And that's when the gates of heaven opened. Let me tell you, it is now a beloved dish in our family. This taco soup is so incredibly good, there have literally been multiple occasions where there was drama in our home about not having enough leftovers for the next day. Trust me, you'll want to make a double batch or even freeze it! I could eat it every week!

1. Heat a large Dutch oven over medium heat. Add the beef and onion and cook until the beef is cooked through, 8 to 10 minutes. Drain off the excess fat.

2. Add the corn, beans, and both tomatoes, with their juices, then add the broth, taco seasoning, and ranch seasoning and bring to a boil. Reduce the heat to low and simmer uncovered for 1 hour.

3. Serve with shredded cheddar, sour cream, corn chips, and green onions.

Serves 10

2 pounds ground beef

1 onion, chopped

Two 15-ounce cans corn kernels, undrained

Two 15-ounce cans ranch-style beans, undrained

Two 14.5-ounce cans petite diced tomatoes, undrained

Two 10-ounce cans Ro-tel mild diced tomatoes and green chiles, undrained

One 14.5-ounce can beef broth

Two 1-ounce packets taco seasoning

Two 1-ounce packets ranch seasoning

FOR SERVING

Shredded cheddar cheese

Sour cream

Corn chips

Chopped green onions

STORAGE

Cool the taco soup, portion into airtight containers (leaving room for expansion), and freeze for up to 4 months. To reheat, thaw overnight in the refrigerator and warm in a saucepan over low heat until heated through.

Mizithra

Serves 4

Kosher salt

16 ounces spaghetti

2 sticks (8 ounces) unsalted butter

1½ cups grated mizithra cheese

Chopped fresh parsley, for serving

Because my mom grew up in a large Italian family of nine, I have a lot of cousins. Whenever there was a special birthday celebration for my grandma or one of my aunts or uncles, we would gather at a restaurant called the Old Spaghetti Factory, because there were so many of us. As a creature of habit, I would always order the same thing: good ol' Mizithra, a pasta dish the restaurant made with a Greek cheese (called mizithra) that's salty and perfect for grating. The combination of rich brown butter drizzled over al dente pasta and mizithra, garnished with chopped parsley, is pure heaven. Even better, this recipe requires only four ingredients, making it an easy-to-make classic dish.

When my mom, Mama Nancy, cracked the code and made a copycat version of the Old Spaghetti Factory's dish, I could not believe it tasted exactly like the original—if not better! With only four ingredients, it's so easy to assemble. Not only can I enjoy as much Mizithra as I want, but I also have control over how much cheese I sprinkle on top. This dish holds more than good flavors and comfort for me—it's like a warm hug of tradition and memories of my beloved Grandma Dodge. I like to think she sends me ladybugs from heaven as a little wink that she's shining down on me.

1. Bring a large pot of salted water to a boil over high heat. Just think of the ocean—your water should be salty like the sea. Add the spaghetti and cook according to the package directions, until al dente. Drain and transfer to a bowl.

2. Meanwhile, in a small saucepan, melt the butter over medium heat and stir frequently until golden brown. Be careful not to burn it. Skim the butter solids off the top and discard.

3. Add the brown butter to the pasta and toss until combined.

4. Top with the shredded mizithra to taste. Mizithra is a salty cheese; use it sparingly. Start with a small amount and adjust to taste. Garnish with chopped parsley and serve.

Monster Burgers

We love celebrating Halloween in our house by creating festive recipes. One of our favorite recipes for October is my son Charlie's Halloween-themed Monster Burgers. To make the burgers, you can use homemade beef patties or opt for store-bought ones. Top the patty with a slice of dill pickle and a slice of cheese with triangular cutouts to resemble teeth. Spread a tablespoon of ketchup over the patty to resemble blood and cover it with a bun. Finally, add two large green olives on toothpicks to create eyes for your monster burgers, giving them an extra spooky touch, and insert them into the bun to complete that monster look. And don't forget to deck them with your favorite toppings. Whether it's crispy bacon, creamy avocado, or a secret sauce, the choice is yours! Remember to remove the toothpicks, especially when serving these to kids.

Serves 4

1 pound ground beef

Kosher salt

4 hamburger buns

Mayonnaise

4 leaves butter lettuce

4 sandwich-sliced pickles

Ketchup

4 slices Swiss cheese

8 pitted green olives or pimento-stuffed olives

1. Divide the ground beef into 4 equal portions and form into patties. Season with salt.

2. Heat a large skillet over medium-high heat and cook until the burgers are well done with no pink, 4 to 5 minutes per side.

3. Toast the buns if desired. For each burger, spread mayo on the bottom bun and top with butter lettuce. Set a cooked burger patty on the lettuce. Arrange a pickle slice to resemble a tongue hanging out of each burger. Cut the Swiss cheese into jagged teeth shapes and layer them along the top edge of the patty. Drizzle ketchup "blood" over the cheese. Top with the top half of the bun.

4. Insert a toothpick into each olive for the eyes and set 2 eyes on each burger.

CELEBRATING TIP

Extend the Halloween fun all month long! Turn any lunch or dinner into a celebration with these easy, festive Monster Burgers.

Jack-o'-Lantern Stuffed Bell Peppers

Serves 4

4 large orange bell peppers (with stems if possible)

1 pound ground beef

1 small onion, diced

Kosher salt and freshly ground black pepper

1 garlic clove, minced

One 6.8-ounce box Rice-A-Roni Beef Flavor

2 tablespoons butter

¼ cup tomato paste

1 tablespoon light brown sugar

1½ cups shredded mozzarella cheese

While candy tends to steal the spotlight during the spooky season, there's more to look forward to than just sweets. I started making these Jack-o'-Lantern Stuffed Bell Peppers five years ago, when Charlie and Claire were little, and to this day, they are our all-time favorite Halloween-themed dinner recipe. I can't wait for them to become one of your family traditions, too. No matter how many years go by, I can't get over how adorable they are. Now you can have your jack-o'-lantern and eat it, too!

1. Preheat the oven to 400°F.

2. Cut the top off each bell pepper and remove the seeds and membranes. Save the tops. Carve jack-'o-lantern faces into each bell pepper.

3. Heat a large skillet over medium heat. Add the ground beef and onion and cook until the beef is cooked through, 8 to 10 minutes. Season with salt and pepper to taste. Add the garlic and cook for an additional 2 minutes. Set aside.

4. Prepare the Rice-A-Roni according to the package directions, using the 2 tablespoons butter the package calls for.

5. In a large bowl, stir together the rice and the beef/onion mixture until combined.

6. In another bowl, stir together the tomato paste, ¼ cup water, and the brown sugar until combined. Stir into the beef/rice mixture.

7. Using a spoon, evenly distribute the mixture among the bell peppers. Top each pepper with mozzarella, then set the reserved bell pepper tops on each stuffed bell pepper to look like a jack-o'-lantern.

recipe continues

APPETIZERS FOR CELEBRATIONS

This chapter is filled with festive and easy-to-make appetizers, great for any celebration—a holiday party, classroom party, after-school snack, birthday party, or simply the everyday. And while it may be tempting to hold on tight to these recipes for a get-together, I encourage you to not wait for a party to make one of these appetizers. Put a little YAY in every day and sprinkle happy memories within the four walls of your home. The ones who matter most are your family. As a fellow memory maker, I can tell you that you will never regret investing the time to celebrate the ones you love most by starting a new tradition or creating a new food memory that will one day become a warm, nostalgic childhood remembrance. Your loved ones will never forget how you made them feel—and these appetizers will surely create happy memories.

Celebrating is about so much more than just perfect party decorations and elaborate events. It runs much deeper. It's about togetherness, cherishing ordinary moments, and finding joy in the simple things. Here's to celebrating daily and creating heartwarming memories that will last a lifetime!

Easter Deviled Eggs

Serves 12

Make happy family food memories with these adorable deviled egg chicks. Whether you're a room parent and need a treat for a classroom party, or you have to take something to an office gathering, or you're hosting your own springtime or Easter celebration, these deviled egg chicks take snack time to a new level of fun.

12 large eggs, hard-boiled and peeled

⅓ cup mayonnaise

2 teaspoons Dijon mustard

Kosher salt

6 black olives

1 carrot

Curly parsley, for garnish

1. Cut a thin slice off the base of each egg to help it stand upright. Slice off the top third of each egg, remove the yolk, and replace the top.

2. In a medium bowl, use a fork to mash together the yolks, mayonnaise, mustard, and salt until combined.

3. Place the mixture in a zip-top bag and snip the tip off one of the bottom corners. Squeeze the mixture into each egg base until it comes ¾ inch out of the top of the egg. Replace the top and lightly press down at an angle, exposing the front of the egg yolk mixture.

4. For the eyes, use a small piping tip or straw to poke out 24 small rounds from the olives. Gently squeeze the straw or tap the piping tip to remove the olive pieces.

5. To create the beaks, slice the carrot into ⅛-inch-thick coins and cut out 24 small triangles.

6. On each deviled egg, arrange 2 olive eyes and 2 stacked carrot triangles for the beak.

7. Arrange the eggs on a serving platter, garnish with fresh parsley, and serve.

Mini Sweet Pepper "Carrots"

Are you searching for a fun and festive appetizer that everyone of all ages will love? Look no further than these family favorite cuties—everyone always talks about how clever these are. You slice mini sweet orange peppers in half lengthwise, add cream cheese, and top off the "carrot" with fresh dill as the "greens." Bonus: You can make these memorable, delicious stuffed peppers ahead of time and refrigerate until ready to serve.

Serves 12

1. Slice each pepper in half lengthwise. With a paring knife, make a small triangular cut to remove each stem, along with the seeds and pith.

2. Fill each pepper half with the cream cheese. Insert a dill sprig into the cream cheese on the top of each pepper to be the carrot greens.

3. Arrange on a serving platter and serve.

12 orange mini sweet peppers

One 12-ounce container chive and onion cream cheese

12 fresh dill sprigs

STORAGE

Prepare this dish up to 24 hours in advance and store it covered in the refrigerator. For the freshest flavor, add the sprigs of dill just before serving.

Tater Puff Skewers

Serves 8

64 frozen Ore-Ida
Tater Tots

Eight 12-inch wooden
skewers

1½ cups shredded
cheddar cheese

⅓ cup store-bought real
bacon bits or chopped
cooked bacon

FOR SERVING

4 green onions, chopped

Ranch dressing

When it comes to Super Bowl Sunday, I'm just cheering for the team my husband, Andy, is cheering for . . . I put on a good front, but in my heart of whole hearts, I'm just here for the food, sofa snuggles, commercials, halftime show, family, and . . . maybe even sneaking off to the stores to go shopping while they're all empty, too!

One of our favorite crowd-pleasing game-day recipes is Tater Puff Skewers! With only four easy ingredients, these skewers are perfect for breakfast, lunch, and dinner—because potatoes are basically hash browns' cousin, and bacon counts for breakfast, too, right? These skewers are the only touchdown I am here for!

1. Preheat the oven to 425°F. Line a baking sheet with parchment paper.

2. Microwave the Tater Tots for 30 seconds to 1 minute to partially thaw them and to ensure they hold their shape on the skewer.

3. Thread 8 Tots onto each of 8 wooden skewers and place in the lined baking sheet. Sprinkle the skewers with the cheddar and bacon bits.

4. Bake until golden brown, 15 to 20 minutes.

5. To serve, top with the chopped green onions, with ranch dressing on the side for dipping.

Cheesy Buffalo Chicken Dip

Packed with shredded chicken, ranch dressing, cream cheese, hot sauce, and loads of melted cheese, this Cheesy Buffalo Chicken Dip has the most mouthwatering Buffalo wing flavor that pairs perfectly with chips or veggie sticks—celery is my favorite for dipping! It's a total crowd-pleaser, and friends and family who try it always end up asking me for the recipe.

Serves 8

1. Heat a large skillet over medium heat. Add the chicken, wings sauce, cream cheese, ranch dressing, and 1 cup of the cheddar. Cook, stirring occasionally, until warmed through and the cream cheese is melted and thoroughly incorporated, about 10 minutes.

2. Preheat the broiler.

3. Place the mixture in a broilerproof 8 × 8-inch baking dish and top with the remaining cheddar. Broil for a few minutes to melt the cheese.

4. Garnish with chopped chives and serve with celery sticks and crackers.

Three 10-ounce cans chicken, drained, or 1¼ cups shredded cooked chicken

¾ cup Frank's RedHot Buffalo Wings Sauce

Two 8-ounce packages cream cheese, at room temperature

1 cup ranch dressing

2 cups shredded cheddar cheese

FOR SERVING

Chopped fresh chives

Celery sticks

Crackers

BLT Dip *with* Potato Chips

Serves 8

1½ cups store-bought real bacon bits or chopped cooked bacon, plus more for garnish

1½ cups mayonnaise

1½ cups sour cream

½ teaspoon onion powder

¾ cup diced tomatoes, plus more for garnish

Chopped lettuce, for garnish

Kettle-cooked potato chips, for serving

BLTs are one of my all-time favorite sandwiches, especially during the summer when I can get fresh tangy tomatoes straight from my father-in-law's garden. At *Best Friends for Frosting*, I LOVE a good recipe twist. Imagine all the flavors of a BLT packed into a creamy and irresistible dip?! I cracked the code, and this BLT dip recipe is guaranteed to be a crowd-pleasing hit! Whether served at a casual block party or even a formal dinner, it truly captures the flavors of a BLT sandwich.

1. In a medium bowl, stir together the bacon bits, mayonnaise, sour cream, and onion powder until well combined. Refrigerate covered for 1 hour to let the flavors incorporate and for the dip to set up.

2. When ready to serve, gently fold in the diced tomatoes. Garnish with additional bacon bits, tomatoes, and lettuce. Serve with potato chips.

Meatball Sliders

Bursting with flavor, these Italian Meatball Sliders are a must-have for game-day celebrations or even for a quick and easy dinner! They remind me so much of the Meatball Marinara Melt, my son Charlie's go-to favorite at Subway. I made these sliders for the first time when Charlie had a sleepover with all his friends, who loved them. I couldn't believe how easy they were to make— you just brush garlic butter on the rolls, cut out meatball-size holes, then fill them with mozzarella, marinara, and your choice of meatballs, whether homemade or precooked and heated—talk about a grocery store shortcut!

Serves 12

4 tablespoons salted butter, melted

3 garlic cloves, minced

12 Hawaiian or dinner rolls (not pulled apart)

12 slices mozzarella cheese

One 12-ounce jar marinara sauce

12 meatballs, thawed if frozen

Chopped fresh flat-leaf parsley, for garnish

1. Preheat the oven to 350°F. Line a baking sheet with parchment paper.

2. In a small bowl, stir together the melted butter and garlic.

3. Brush the bottom of the rolls with half of the garlic butter. Place the rolls on the lined baking sheet. Cut out a meatball-size hole in the top of each roll with a paring knife, keeping the bottoms of the rolls intact. Brush the top of each roll with the remaining garlic butter.

4. Fold up one slice of mozzarella cheese and add to the bottom of each cut-out roll. Fill each roll with a spoonful of marinara sauce, a meatball, and another spoonful of sauce.

5. Bake until the meatballs are heated, 15 to 20 minutes.

6. Garnish with chopped parsley and serve.

Mummy Dogs

Celebrating doesn't have to mean making festive treats only on the actual holiday. I always have so much fun surprising the kids with easy Halloween food ideas sprinkled throughout the month of October. These Mummy Dogs are in my October meal-planning rotation every year—and the comfort of repeating traditions lives on. It doesn't matter how many years go by—this appetizer is as cute as I thought it was the first year I started making it. This Halloween treat is so easy to make: it's just refrigerated crescent rolls, hot dogs, and eyeball sprinkles (see Tip).

Serves 8

One 8-ounce can Pillsbury Crescent Rolls

8 hot dogs

Mustard, plus more for serving

16 eyeball sprinkles (optional; see Tip)

Ketchup, for serving

1. Preheat the oven to 375°F. Line a baking sheet with parchment paper.

2. Roll out the crescent dough and use a knife or pizza cutter to cut it into ¼-inch-wide strips.

3. Wrap each hot dog with dough strips overlapping each other to resemble a mummy. Leave a small space on the end of the hot dog for the candy eyes. Arrange the mummy dogs on the lined baking sheet.

4. Bake for about 15 minutes, or until golden brown.

5. When they are cool enough to handle, add 2 beads of mustard and attach 2 eyeball sprinkles to each mummy dog.

6. Serve with ketchup and mustard for dipping.

QUICK TIP

Instead of edible eyeballs, you can easily place a dot of ketchup or mustard you likely already have on hand in the kitchen.

Jack-o'-Lantern Taco Dip

Serves 8

½ pound lean ground beef

½ cup diced onion

2 jalapeños, minced

2 tablespoons chili powder

2 teaspoons ground cumin

1 cup mayonnaise

One 8-ounce package cream cheese

2½ cups shredded cheddar cheese

One 10-ounce can Ro-tel mild diced tomatoes and green chiles, drained

FOR DECORATION

1 jalapeño

3 blue tortilla chips, plus more for serving

13 black olive slices

I'm always so excited to make the Halloween season extra spook-tacular with this fun and festive jack-o'-lantern dip. Fill a round pie dish with taco filling, top with cheese, and bake in the oven. Complete the look with blue corn tortilla chips for the eyes and nose, a jalapeño for the stem, and olive slices for the mouth. It's cheesy and warm and combines beef and nacho cheese flavors. Give this taco dip recipe a try and create a memorable dish for your family!

1. Preheat the oven to 375°F.

2. Heat a medium skillet over medium-high heat. Add the ground beef and cook until browned, about 10 minutes. Drain off any excess fat.

3. Add the onion, jalapeños, chili powder, and cumin and cook until the onion is slightly translucent, 2 to 3 minutes.

4. Stir in the mayonnaise, cream cheese, 1 cup of the cheddar, and the canned diced tomatoes. Transfer to a 9-inch pie dish. Top with the remaining 1½ cups shredded cheddar.

5. Bake until the cheese is melted, about 10 minutes.

6. To decorate: Slice the jalapeño to separate the stem cap from the pepper. Arrange 2 blue chips on the taco dip for the eyes, half of a chip for the nose, and olive slices for the mouth. Top with the jalapeño stem cap, for the jack-o'-lantern stem.

7. For the best gooey-cheese effect, aim to serve within 20 minutes of taking it out of the oven. Serve with blue tortilla chips.

Halloween Dip

Does your family embrace the spooky or silly side of Halloween? At our house, we like having the best of both worlds, and it shines through in our snacks and meals. While not every meal is meant to be spooky, I love adding fun details that surprise my kids or make them laugh. The last time I made this Halloween appetizer, I couldn't resist and ate half before the kids got home from school. It's packed with different layers of flavor, making it an enticing Halloween snack. It may have a Halloween-inspired appearance with a "web" of sour cream, but it's a delightful recipe that can be enjoyed all year round.

Serves 8

Three 16-ounce cans refried beans

¼ cup taco seasoning

3 cups guacamole

½ cup sour cream

1 tomato, diced

½ cup shredded cheddar or Mexican-blend cheese

½ cup sliced black olives

4 green onions, chopped

Warmed tortilla chips, for serving

1. In a medium bowl, stir together the refried beans and taco seasoning.

2. Spread the refried beans into a single layer along the bottom of a 9-inch pie dish. Spread the guacamole into a layer over the refried beans.

3. To create the spider web, pipe 2 perpendicular lines of the sour cream using a squeeze bottle or piping bag. Divide each section two more times to create a total of 16 sections. Pipe 2 small half circles across each section to create the outer and inner rows of the web.

4. Arrange the diced tomato, shredded cheese, olives, and green onions around the perimeter of the dip, and add a plastic spider in the center for some fun.

5. Serve with warm tortilla chips.

Pumpkin Cheese Ball

Serves 8

Two 8-ounce packages cream cheese, at room temperature

3 cups finely shredded cheddar cheese

4 green onions, chopped

1 bell pepper stem

Crackers, for serving

This Pumpkin Cheese Ball is a fun memory-making treat for celebrating every day in fall, Halloween, or even Thanksgiving. It's a showstopper on any table! It's creamy and savory, with a sharp kick from the cheddar cheese and a fresh hint of green onion! It's a festive after-school snack, party appetizer, or even a fun activity with the kids. All you have to do is spread plastic wrap on a surface and layer cheese ball batter on top of shredded cheese. Shape the cheese ball into a pumpkin using kitchen twine to create pumpkin-like indentations. Chill the cheese ball, remove the twine, and add a bell pepper stem for a finished pumpkin appearance. Serve this cheese ball with your favorite crackers or fresh veggies. And if you love this recipe, you can easily make it into a snowman (see page 83) using a blend of Monterey Jack and cheddar.

1. In a medium bowl, stir together the cream cheese, 1½ cups of the cheddar, and the green onions until well combined.

2. Form the mixture into a ball. Roll the cheese ball in the remaining 1½ cups cheddar and wrap it with plastic wrap. Tie the cheese ball with four pieces of twine to create the pumpkin lines and refrigerate for 1 hour.

3. Remove the twine, unwrap the cheese ball, and gently press a bell pepper stem into the top center of the pumpkin.

4. Serve with crackers.

Snowman Cheese Ball

It's hard to believe I've only experienced snow a handful of times, but I'll always adore a festive snowman treat. This adorable snowman Christmas appetizer is made with creamy cream cheese, ranch seasoning, and a blend of cheddar and Monterey Jack cheese, making it a showstopping hit at any holiday gathering. Serve with crackers and a cheese knife for spreading, and watch as your guests delight in this cheesy masterpiece!

Serves 8

1. In a large bowl, stir together the cream cheese, ranch seasoning, and cheddar cheese until well combined.

2. Using plastic wrap, shape one-third of the mixture into a ball to create the head of the snowman. Unwrap the snowman's head and roll it in the finely shredded Monterey Jack cheese. Rewrap it with plastic wrap and reshape it back into a ball if necessary.

3. Repeat with the remaining two-thirds of the mixture to form the snowman's body. Refrigerate the cheese balls for 2 to 3 hours, until firm.

4. Unwrap each cheese ball. Carefully cut 2 wooden skewers in half and insert the 4 skewer halves into the top of the snowman's body, leaving some of the skewer sticking out. Using the exposed skewer ends, attach the head to the body.

5. Press the whole peppercorns into the cheese balls to create the snowman's eyes, mouth, and buttons. Insert half of a baby carrot into the head for the snowman's nose.

6. Serve with crackers and a cheese knife for spreading.

Two 8-ounce packages cream cheese, at room temperature

One 1-ounce packet ranch seasoning

3 cups finely shredded cheddar cheese

2 cups finely shredded Monterey Jack cheese

2 wooden skewers

14 black peppercorns

1 baby carrot, halved

Crackers, for serving

Santa Veggie Board

Serves 10

One 10-ounce container hummus

1 head cauliflower

2 red bell peppers

11 mozzarella balls

Two 15-ounce cans pitted large black olives, drained

1¼ cups cherry tomatoes

2 cucumbers, sliced into rounds

1½ cups almonds

1½ cups gherkin pickles

Jingle your way over and indulge in the cutest veggie board ever! Bring the holiday spirit to life at home by decking the halls with veggies and creating a memorable after-school snack or holiday party appetizer. When I was growing up, my mom always made the holidays extra special by creating happy food memories. This joyful crudités platter is simple and festive for a Christmas celebration. It's packed with a variety of healthy ingredients like hummus, fresh veggies, olives, pickles, mozzarella, and almonds, so both kids and adults will relish snacking on this fun-filled Santa board.

1. Place the container of hummus in the center of a large rectangular platter. This will be Santa's face.

2. Cut the cauliflower into small florets and arrange around the bottom of the hummus to create Santa's beard.

3. Cut the bell peppers into thin strips and arrange on the top half of the platter to make Santa's hat.

4. Place 4 mozzarella balls at the tip of the hat and 6 balls around the base of the hat.

5. Cut an olive in half lengthwise to create Santa's eyes, then cut 2 thin crescents of mozzarella for his eyebrows, a halved cherry tomato for his nose, and a bell pepper piece for his mouth.

6. Arrange the rest of the ingredients around Santa and serve.

Broccoli Christmas Tree

I feel like I am always on a diet around the holidays, and then somehow I break it, crack a joke, and say "diet starts Monday." Deck the halls with boughs of broccoli, with this easy and nutritious six-ingredient Christmas veggie tray . . . I mean tree! It's the perfect treat to bring to keep yourself on track at holiday parties and get-togethers in a healthy way. It takes only 10 minutes to prep, simply arranging broccoli as the tree, yellow peppers as the star topper, cherry tomatoes as the colorful ornaments, and mini pretzel sticks as the trunk. Add some ranch dressing and hummus, and you'll have an adorable and refreshing appetizer for your holiday party. *Deck the dishes with boughs of broccoli, fa la la la la la la la la laaaa!*

Serves 8

4 cups fresh broccoli florets

1 pint cherry tomatoes

2 yellow bell peppers, thinly sliced

10 mini pretzel sticks, plus more for serving

FOR SERVING

Ranch dressing

Hummus

1. On a rectangular serving platter, arrange 1 row of broccoli for the base of the Christmas tree, leaving a few inches of space at the bottom.

2. Arrange a row of cherry tomatoes above the broccoli to resemble a garland.

3. Add 3 more rows of broccoli, tapering up with each row to create the Christmas tree shape.

4. Arrange another row of cherry tomatoes above the broccoli.

5. Add 3 to 4 more rows of broccoli, gradually tapering upward to the point of the Christmas tree.

6. Arrange 3 or 4 yellow bell pepper slices crosswise on top of the broccoli tree to resemble a star.

7. Arrange the pretzel sticks at the bottom of the tree to create the tree trunk.

8. Serve immediately, with ranch dressing and hummus for dipping and the remaining veggies and pretzels on the side.

Ranch Snack Mix

Serves 10

6 cups Rice Chex cereal

3 cups cheese crackers (half regular cheddar, half white cheddar)

2 cups pretzels

2 cups oyster crackers

2 cups dry roasted peanuts

8 tablespoons (1 stick) unsalted butter

One 1-ounce packet ranch seasoning

½ cup grated parmesan cheese

1 tablespoon dried parsley flakes

STORAGE

Store in an airtight container at room temperature for up to 4 days.

There's nothing I love more than snuggling up with my kids and reliving the magic of my favorite childhood movies. If you grew up in the '90s, you might remember classics like *Freaky Friday*, *Matilda*, *Beethoven*, *Hocus Pocus*, and *The Sandlot*—those were the days! Now my kids pile into my bed for epic sleepovers to watch those same movies. And no movie night is complete without the star of the snack table (or bed!), like this savory, crunchy, salty, cheesy Ranch Snack Mix. The combo of airy Chex, crisp pretzels, buttery crackers, and peanuts, all coated in zesty ranch seasoning and parmesan, is simply irresistible and brings a burst of fun and flavor to every bite.

1. Preheat the oven to 300°F. Line a large baking sheet with parchment paper.

2. In a large bowl, gently mix together the Rice Chex, cheese crackers, pretzels, oyster crackers, and peanuts.

3. Spread the mixture onto the lined baking sheet.

4. In a small microwave-safe bowl, melt the butter in the microwave. Drizzle the melted butter evenly over the mixture on the baking sheet. Mix to combine.

5. Sprinkle the ranch seasoning, parmesan cheese, and parsley flakes evenly over the mixture. Gently mix to coat and spread into a thin, even layer.

6. Bake for about 16 minutes, or until golden brown.

7. Let cool for 10 minutes before serving.

Celebrating holidays

and seasons is my

love language

Slow Cooker Cranberry Meatballs

Serves 12

One 48-ounce family-size bag frozen homestyle meatballs

One 18-ounce bottle BBQ sauce

One 14-ounce can jellied cranberry sauce

Fresh cranberries, for garnish (optional)

Rosemary sprigs, for garnish (optional)

This recipe is one of my all-time favorite party appetizers and always a hit at my husband Andy's family parties! I can still remember checking the slow cooker to notice they were all gone, feeling a spark of disappointment that I wouldn't get a plate myself, but also a sense of joy that they were enjoyed by others. An empty serving dish is the best compliment! They're a breeze to whip up, thanks to the convenience of frozen meatballs and cranberries. Place the ingredients in the pot to cook and keep warm throughout the day—you will have happy tummies and memories, and your house will smell wonderful.

1. Add the meatballs, BBQ sauce, and cranberry sauce to a slow cooker and cook on high for 3 hours, stirring occasionally. (Alternatively, if you do not have a slow cooker, set a large pot over medium heat. Add the frozen meatballs, BBQ sauce, and cranberry sauce, mix to combine, and bring to a simmer, covered. Reduce the heat to low and simmer until the meatballs are heated through, stirring occasionally to make sure they cook evenly, 30 to 35 minutes.)

2. Allow the meatballs to cool slightly and serve warm. Garnish with fresh cranberries and rosemary, if using.

STORAGE

Cool the meatballs in the slow cooker, then transfer them to an airtight container and refrigerate for up to 4 days. To reheat, warm gently on the stovetop over medium-low heat or in a slow cooker on low for a few hours.

Brie, Apple, *and* Honey Crostini

Elevate your everyday with these easy yet oh-so-elegant crostini. We're talking warm, toasty baguette slices topped with creamy Brie, crisp apple slices, and crunchy pecans. A drizzle of honey and a squeeze of lemon juice bring it all together, making these little bites irresistible. Talk about a total flavor explosion! They're so simple to whip up that you'll find any excuse to celebrate— from a Tuesday night treat to a weekend gathering with friends, these crostini are guaranteed to add a touch of magic to the ordinary.

Serves 8

1 baguette, cut into ½-inch slices

8 ounces Brie cheese, cut into thin slices

2 large apples, halved, cored, and thinly sliced

Juice of 1 lemon

½ cup chopped pecans

Honey, for drizzling

1. Preheat the oven to 425°F. Line a baking sheet with parchment paper.

2. Place the baguette slices on the lined baking sheet. Top each with a slice of Brie.

3. Bake for about 6 minutes, or until the cheese is melted and the bread is toasted.

4. While the crostini are baking, toss the apple slices in the lemon juice.

5. Remove the crostini from the oven and top with the apple slices and chopped pecans. Drizzle with honey and serve immediately.

WALKING TREATS

Snack time is about to get a whole lot more fun! This chapter reimagines your favorite treats as easy, handheld delights eaten straight from the packaging. In the true spirit of celebrating every day, I'll show you how to transform ordinary bags of chips or cookies into the cutest portable handheld treats you ever did see. Picture picnics with Walking Strawberry Pretzel Salad (page 98), campfire fun with Walking S'Mores (page 94), and tailgating it up with Walking Doritos Tacos (page 102). As I take a walk down memory lane, I can still remember the snacks packaging and labels from my own childhood. Isn't it funny how they still look nearly the same after all these years?! Even as an adult, I get nostalgic comfort from the familiarity of those packaged treats.

And did I mention there are so many fun ways to customize these handheld treats for parties?! Add a toppings bar with sprinkles, serve them with colored forks to match your theme, or even set up a self-serve bar for taco toppings!

Whether you whip up Walking Treats for a special occasion or to celebrate the everyday, they will bring joy to both kids and adults alike! Just grab a fork and dig in straight from the bag. Now that's what I call all walk and no talk!

Walking S'Mores

Serves 10

12 snack-pack bags Honey Teddy Grahams

10 individual chocolate pudding cups

1 cup mini marshmallows

¾ cup milk chocolate chips

Walking S'mores are a fun twist on the classic s'mores without needing a campfire. Did I mention this dessert comes together in 5 minutes, making it an easy handheld treat for summer or fall? And the best part? They are mess-free, so there is no need to worry about sticky fingers—just open individual bags of Teddy Grahams and spoon in chocolate pudding to make them. Then, add mini marshmallows and milk chocolate chips. This recipe is easily scalable, so feel free to add as much or as few of the ingredients as your heart desires.

1. Open 10 bags of Teddy Grahams, reserving 2 bags for garnish.

2. Place the opened bags in a serving tray or baking dish to prop them up. Spoon a pudding cup into each of the bags. Divide the marshmallows and chocolate chips among the bags.

3. Top with the reserved Teddy Grahams. Serve with spoons and enjoy!

There's something truly magical about the taste of a recipe from your childhood

Walking
Cookies *and* Cream

Whether it's a hot spring or summer day or you're hosting a pool party, celebrating a birthday, or simply enjoying the everyday sunshine, make this easy handheld treat to sprinkle extra joy over the ones you care about most. You only need bags of mini Oreo cookies, your favorite ice cream, and traditional sundae toppings like whipped cream, sprinkles, and maraschino cherries.

Serves 10

1. Open 10 bags of mini Oreos, reserving 2 bags for garnish.
2. Place the opened bags in a serving tray or baking dish to prop them up.
3. Keeping the 2 reserved bags sealed, lightly crush the Oreos with a rolling pin.
4. Add a scoop of ice cream to each of the 10 opened Oreos bags and sprinkle the crushed Oreos around the ice cream.
5. Top with whipped cream, sprinkles, and a cherry. Serve with spoons and enjoy!

12 bags mini Oreos

10 scoops vanilla ice cream

Whipped cream

Sprinkles

10 maraschino cherries

CELEBRATING TIP

Set up a sundae topping bar and allow loved ones to customize with their favorite flavors to make the ultimate treat!

Walking
Strawberry Pretzel Salad

Serves 10

Inspired by my husband Andy's Grandma Arlene's family-favorite Strawberry Jell-O Pretzel Salad (page 140), this handheld version combines the familiar flavors of cheesecake pudding, strawberries, whipped cream, and pretzels. This is a fun and portable go-anywhere snack. It's a fruity addition to summer picnics, BBQs, graduation parties, baby showers, and more.

One 3.4-ounce package instant cheesecake pudding mix

2 cups cold milk

Twelve 1-ounce bags mini pretzels

One 21-ounce can strawberry pie filling

One 8-ounce container Cool Whip or other whipped cream topping

1. In a medium bowl, whisk together the pudding mix and milk. Place in the refrigerator to set according to the package directions.

2. Keeping the pretzel bags closed, gently crush the pretzels with a rolling pin. Set 2 bags aside for garnish.

3. Open 10 bags and place them in a serving tray or baking dish to prop them up. Fill each of the opened bags with pudding and strawberry pie filling.

4. Top with Cool Whip and garnish with the reserved crushed pretzels. Serve with spoons and enjoy!

CELEBRATING TIP

Don't wait for a holiday or special occasion to picnic or barbecue. Sprinkle extra joy over the ones you love most by having an impromptu picnic or barbecue just because. I remember my parents doing this, and the level of excitement was always 10/10! It's all about taking the ordinary to extraordinary to make happy memories! I promise you will never regret it.

Walking
Chili Cheese Fritos

Walking Chili Cheese Fritos take ordinary chili to extraordinary chili. Start with mini bags of Frito corn chips and layer with savory chili and melted cheese. Display toppings such as sour cream, jalapeño slices, and chopped green onions, and let loved ones fill their Walking Fritos up with their favorite toppings. Grab a fork and dig right on in!

Serves 12

1. In a large microwave-safe bowl, microwave the chili for 2 minutes.

2. Open the bags of Fritos. Remove half of the chips from each bag and set aside.

3. Place the bags in a serving tray or baking dish to prop them up. Divide half of the warmed chili evenly into the Fritos bags and top with 2 cups of the cheese. Add the reserved Fritos, the other half of the chili, and the remaining cheese.

4. Top each with pickled jalapeños, a dollop of sour cream, and chopped green onions. Serve with forks and dig in!

Two 15-ounce cans chili

Twelve 1-ounce bags Fritos corn chips

3 cups shredded cheddar cheese

¾ cup pickled jalapeño slices

One 8-ounce container sour cream

½ cup chopped green onions

Walking Doritos Tacos

Serves 10

2 pounds ground beef

1 medium onion, diced

Two 1-ounce packets taco seasoning

Ten 1-ounce bags Nacho Cheese Doritos

2 cups shredded cheddar cheese

1½ cups shredded lettuce

¾ cup guacamole

¾ cup sour cream

½ cup pickled jalapeño slices

½ cup chopped green onions

½ cup chopped fresh cilantro

Walking tacos are the real MVPs, as they're the original walking treat that sparked the inspiration behind this entire chapter of walking treats. When I make these at home for our family of four, I can easily customize them since I know my daughter, Claire, isn't a fan of tomatoes, onions, or jalapeños, while my husband, Andy, and son, Charlie, enjoy all the toppings.

When hosting multiple people, it's best to set up a walking taco bar. Not only is it interactive, but it also allows everyone to customize their toppings to their preferences and even avoid soggy produce. Plus, it's one less chore you will have on your plate . . . I mean bag! For your taco bar, prepare a variety of toppings, such as cheese, shredded lettuce, guacamole, sour cream, pickled jalapeños, green onions, and cilantro. Display the bags of Nacho Cheese Doritos and prepared taco meat for your guests and offer plenty of forks and napkins. It's also helpful to have a visual sample bag to show guests how to assemble theirs.

1. Heat a large skillet over medium heat. Add the ground beef and onion and cook until the beef is browned, 8 to 10 minutes. Stir in the taco seasoning.

2. Keeping the bags sealed, lightly crush each bag of chips with a rolling pin. Open the bags and place in a serving tray or baking dish to prop them up.

3. When ready to serve, set out bowls of the beef mixture, cheese, shredded lettuce, guacamole, sour cream, pickled jalapeños, green onions, and cilantro next to the tray of bags. Let everyone assemble their own. Serve with forks, and let them have at it!

You can still throw
confetti and miss the life
you used to have

Walking "Dirt *and* Worms"

When I was growing up, my dad would get grossed out by the word "worm." My brothers and I were not allowed to say it, but we had to call it the "W" word if we did. Even that would make him lose his appetite, mainly if he ate spaghetti. As an adult, this story makes me chuckle a bit. And maybe the rebel in me secretly mischievously chuckles as I make this recipe with the kids because I know this would not have flown at home. These bags are made with a layer of chocolate pudding and crushed Oreo cookies for the "dirt" and then topped with gummy worms. You can give this treat an even spookier effect by adding candy eyes. Whether you're a kid at heart, a parent, a grandparent, the world's best auntie or uncle, or a schoolteacher, these make for a fun Halloween snack.

Serves 10

Twelve 1-ounce bags mini Oreos

12 individual chocolate pudding cups

24 gummy worms, cut in half

36 eyeball sprinkles

1. Open 10 bags of mini Oreos, reserving 2 bags for the "dirt."

2. Place the opened bags in a serving tray or baking dish to prop them up.

3. Keeping the 2 reserved bags sealed, crush the Oreos with a rolling pin to create the "dirt." (We're talking the kind of dirt that is so good, it'll make you dig for more!)

4. Evenly divide the chocolate pudding into the 10 opened Oreo bags. Top each with Oreo "dirt," worms, and eyeballs.

5. Serve with a spoon to shovel in some sweetness. Who knew digging for worms could be so delicious? (Yes, I am talking to you, Dad! ;))

Walking
Banana Cream Pie

Serves 10

One 3.4-ounce package
instant banana cream
pudding mix

2 cups cold milk

Twelve 1-ounce bags
mini Nilla wafers

Whipped cream

3 bananas, thinly sliced

10 maraschino cherries

These handheld banana cream "pies" are fabulous for celebrating everyday moments and sunny days ahead. The yellow packaging adds a beautiful pop of color to any joyful party. They are a creamy and fruity twist on the classic banana pudding dessert, and you only need six ingredients to bust out the fun! All that's required are some bags of mini Nilla wafers, sliced bananas, banana pudding, whipped cream, and toppings, like a cherry or even sprinkles, for a fun and festive presentation. Grab a fork and enjoy these delightful treats straight out of the bag. It's that easy!

1   In a medium bowl, whisk together the pudding mix and milk. Place in the refrigerator to set according to the package directions.

2   Open 10 bags of mini Nilla wafers, reserving 2 bags for garnish.

3   Place the opened bags in a serving tray or baking dish to prop them up. Evenly divide the pudding, whipped cream, and sliced bananas among the bags.

4   Garnish with the reserved bags of mini Nilla wafers and a maraschino cherry. Serve immediately with spoons.

Walking Chocolate Cream Pie

Serves 10

This treat is a fun twist on the classic Oreo pie, a combination of creamy chocolate pudding, crunchy cookies, fluffy whipped cream, and chocolate chips that will excite all your favorite chocolate lovers.

One 3.4-ounce package instant chocolate pudding mix

2 cups cold milk

Twelve 1-ounce bags mini Keebler Fudge Stripe Cookies

Whipped cream

1 cup chocolate chips

1. In a medium bowl, whisk together the pudding mix and milk. Place in the refrigerator to set according to the package directions.

2. Open 10 bags of Fudge Stripe cookies, reserving 2 bags for garnish.

3. Place the opened bags in a serving tray or baking dish to prop them up. Evenly divide the pudding and whipped cream among the bags.

4. Garnish with the chocolate chips and reserved 2 bags of cookies. Serve with spoons.

CELEBRATING TIP

Add colorful sprinkles to make this treat extra festive for a birthday or any other special occasion.

Walking Chocolate Peanut Butter Dessert

These chocolate peanut butter treats combine the perfect balance of sweet and salty flavors. All you need is mini Nutter Butter cookies, chocolate pudding, mini chocolate chips, and whipped cream! And for an extra pop of color, add sprinkles— totally optional. Keep smiling and making those sweet memories with the ones you love most!

Serves 10

1. In a medium bowl, whisk together the pudding mix and milk. Place in the refrigerator to set according to the package directions.

2. Open 10 bags of Nutter Butter cookies, reserving 2 bags for garnish.

3. Remove half of the cookies from each open bag and place the bags in a serving tray or baking dish to prop them up. Place a few tablespoons of pudding on top of the cookies in each bag, then add the remaining cookies, then another layer of pudding.

4. Top with whipped cream and garnish with the mini chocolate chips and reserved Nutter Butter cookies. Serve with spoons and enjoy!

One ¾-ounce package instant chocolate pudding mix

2 cups cold milk

Twelve 1-ounce packages mini Nutter Butter cookies

Whipped cream

½ cup mini chocolate chips

TIME-SAVING DESSERT SHORTCUTS

What if I told you there was a way to make an enjoyable dessert that took only minutes to prepare, allowing you to make the most of every season, celebration, or special occasion? It's a busy bee's recipe for success! Filled with time-saving dessert shortcuts, this chapter features recipes that combine fresh ingredients with store-bought shortcuts, resulting in mouthwatering desserts prepared in minutes that taste like they were made completely from scratch.

From simple no-bake hacks like my Ice Cream Sandwich Cake (page 113) to two-ingredient shortcuts like Chocolate Chip Cookie Cinnamon Rolls (page 117) to adding Cool Whip and fresh berries to a store-bought angel food cake (see page 126), this chapter is filled to the brim with easy shortcuts that once again prove "done is better than perfect!"

Ice Cream Sandwich Cake

I often joke this cake got me on the Jerry Springer show because Daphne Oz featured it on her show, *The Good Dish*'s "Ice Cream Episode," and Jerry Springer came on the same episode to make an ice cream sundae. That counts, right?!

I call this the ultimate easy birthday cake because you literally just have to assemble it, pop it in the freezer for a few hours, and serve it. You can even make it a few days ahead. Whether you're celebrating the first day of summer or a birthday party, this four-ingredient frozen ice cream cake is too easy to prepare, making it one of my all-time favorite time-saving dessert shortcuts. It has become one of our happiest birthday traditions for many of our followers at *Best Friends for Frosting*.

Serves 16

24 ice cream sandwiches

One 16-ounce container Cool Whip

2 cups mini M&M's

Sprinkles

1. In a 9 × 13-inch baking dish, create a single layer of ice cream sandwiches. If needed, cut the ice cream sandwiches to fit.

2. Spread half of the Cool Whip over the ice cream sandwiches, then sprinkle with half of the M&M's.

3. Add a second layer of ice cream sandwiches, Cool Whip, and the remaining M&M's, then top with sprinkles.

4. Place in the freezer for 2 to 3 hours to set.

STORAGE

Store the cake in an airtight container in the freezer. When ready to serve, remove and let sit on the counter for up to 25 minutes before serving and slicing. For best results, enjoy this ice cream sandwich cake within a week.

CELEBRATING TIP

The personalization options are endless, as you can use nearly ANY chocolate-based candy for this recipe. Have a blast getting creative with chocolate candies that are customized to the birthday boy's or girl's favorites! Even better, customize for any holiday or season! Use red and blue M&M's for Fourth of July, pastels for Easter, black and orange for Halloween, and green for Saint Patrick's Day.

Heavy Cream Cinnamon Rolls

Serves 10

Two 17.5-ounce cans Pillsbury Grands! Cinnamon Rolls with Icing

1¼ cups heavy cream

1 stick (4 ounces) unsalted butter, melted

1¼ cups packed light brown sugar

1 teaspoon ground cinnamon

If you're looking for an easy crowd-pleasing recipe that's perfect for holidays, desserts, or even a special weekday treat, my Heavy Cream Cinnamon Rolls recipe is a keeper! It's a super-easy shortcut to transform a basic can of cinnamon rolls with just cream, brown sugar, and butter into pure decadence. I've spent countless hours perfecting this recipe, and it's become a beloved tradition in my family—it's always the first thing to disappear! It's one of my go-to recipes for holiday parties, a total must-have for holiday breakfasts, and even a happy surprise for the morning after sleepovers.

1. Preheat the oven to 350°F.

2. Arrange the cinnamon rolls in a 9 × 13-inch baking dish. Pour the heavy cream evenly over the cinnamon rolls.

3. In a medium bowl, stir together the melted butter, brown sugar, and cinnamon until combined. Pour the mixture over the cinnamon rolls. Cover with foil.

4. Bake for 40 minutes, or until golden brown.

5. Let cool for 20 minutes. Warm the packaged icing in the microwave for 15 seconds, then drizzle over the rolls and serve.

CELEBRATING TIP

Keep all the ingredients on hand to easily whip these heavy cream cinnamon rolls up for a special celebration at the very last minute. Bonus: Your house will smell AMAZING!

Chocolate Chip Cookie Cinnamon Rolls

Two-ingredient Chocolate Chip Cookie Cinnamon Rolls are among the best shortcut desserts ever! All you need is a can of cinnamon rolls and a pack of chocolate chip cookie dough. I've made countless recipes over the years, and this is hands down one of my absolute favorites. Who would have thought you could combine a can of cinnamon rolls with a package of cookie dough?!

Serves 10

Flour, for sprinkling

One 16-ounce tube refrigerated chocolate chip cookie dough (preferably Pillsbury)

One 17.5-ounce can Pillsbury Grands! Cinnamon Rolls with Icing

1. Preheat the oven to 350°F. Line a baking sheet with parchment paper.

2. Sprinkle a cutting board with flour and roll out the chocolate chip cookie dough into a 5 × 9-inch rectangle ½ inch thick.

3. Unroll each cinnamon roll and arrange the strips lengthwise over the cookie dough rectangle. Trim any excess cinnamon roll dough at the ends of the cookie dough rectangle and reincorporate the excess dough where needed. Use a pizza cutter or a knife to cut the dough lengthwise into 10 strips.

4. Flip each strip of cookie dough so the cinnamon roll side is on the bottom. Gently roll each dough strip back up into a roll and press the end of the cinnamon roll dough in to seal it. Arrange the rolls 1 to 2 inches apart on the lined baking sheet.

5. Bake for 20 to 25 minutes, or until golden brown.

6. Let cool on a cooling rack for 10 minutes. Warm the packaged icing in the microwave for 15 seconds, then drizzle over the rolls and serve.

SPRINKLE HAPPY

MEMORIES LIKE

CONFETTI

Cinnamon Roll Apple Pies

Cinnamon Roll Apple Pies are a simple and satisfying dessert you can make in a snap! Quickly whip up this sweet treat with just two ingredients—cinnamon rolls and apple pie filling. Full disclosure: Your house is about to smell better than a Bath & Body Works candle in the best way imaginable.

Serves 8

1. Preheat the oven to 400°F. Grease 8 cups of a muffin tin with cooking spray.

2. Add one cinnamon roll per muffin cup and push down in the center to make a bowl shape. Fill each cinnamon roll with apple pie filling.

3. Bake for 15 to 20 minutes, until golden brown.

4. Let cool for 10 minutes. Warm the packaged icing in the microwave for 15 seconds, then drizzle over the rolls.

Cooking spray

One 8-ounce can Pillsbury Cinnamon Rolls with Icing

One 21-ounce can apple pie filling

Apple Pie Bites

Serves 8

With just a few simple ingredients, you can create a comforting and irresistible treat that captures all the flavors of a classic apple pie without the trouble of making it! The combination of warm, buttery, flaky crescent roll dough, sweet apple pie filling, pecans with a satisfying crunch, and a hint of pumpkin spice creates a memorable fall treat that is hard to resist.

¼ cup packed light brown sugar

1 teaspoon pumpkin pie spice

1 Granny Smith apple

3 tablespoons unsalted butter, melted

One 8-ounce can Pillsbury Crescent Rolls

⅓ cup chopped pecans

1. Preheat the oven to 375°F. Line a baking sheet with parchment paper.

2. In a small bowl, stir together the brown sugar and pumpkin pie spice until combined.

3. Cut the unpeeled apple into 8 wedges and trim out the core (I like to use an apple slicer to make things simple). In a small bowl, toss the apple wedges with 2 tablespoons of the melted butter.

4. Unroll and separate the crescent roll dough and arrange the triangles on the lined baking sheet. Evenly sprinkle the brown sugar mixture and pecans over each triangle.

5. Place an apple wedge on the wide end of each crescent roll and roll the dough around each wedge. Brush each crescent roll with the remaining 1 tablespoon melted butter.

6. Bake for 10 to 12 minutes, until the crescents are golden brown.

7. Let cool for 5 minutes before serving.

Easy Berry Cake

This dessert almost feels like cheating because it's so easy to make and it's packed with sweet flavor. Just dump blueberries and strawberries into a baking dish and drizzle with lemon juice. Top it all off with sugar, white cake mix, and sliced butter. Pop it in the oven and start baking memories. Take it to the next level by serving it warm with a scoop of vanilla ice cream.

Serves 8

1. Preheat the oven to 350°F.

2. Spread the blueberries and strawberries into an even layer in a 9 × 13-inch baking dish. Drizzle with the lemon juice.

3. Sprinkle the sugar and white cake mix over the berries to coat evenly.

4. Evenly space slices of butter on top of the cake mix.

5. Bake for about 45 minutes, or until the top of the cake turns golden brown and a toothpick or knife inserted in the center comes out clean.

6. Scoop individual portions with a serving spoon. Serve warm with vanilla ice cream.

3 cups frozen blueberries

3 cups frozen strawberries

2 tablespoons lemon juice

½ cup sugar

One 14.25-ounce box white cake mix

1½ sticks (6 ounces) butter, cut into ¼-inch-thick slices

Vanilla ice cream, for serving

CELEBRATING TIP

Keep these ingredients on hand for spontaneous occasions. This recipe is famous for its simplicity and enjoyability for a reason.

Lemon Cheesecake Crescent Rolls

Serves 8

Cooking spray

One 8-ounce can
Pillsbury Crescent Rolls

One 24.3-ounce tub
Philadelphia No Bake
Cheesecake Filling

½ cup lemon curd

Powdered sugar,
for serving

My Grandma Dodge's favorite dessert was anything lemon. Whenever I eat something lemon-flavored, like these bite-size desserts with tangy lemon curd, I always happily remember her. My secret ingredient that our followers at *Best Friends for Frosting* are always surprised to learn about is Philadelphia's No Bake Cheesecake Filling. You can find it in the dairy section at the grocery store, next to the containers of cream cheese.

1. Preheat the oven to 350°F. Grease 8 cups of a muffin tin with cooking spray.

2. Unroll and separate the crescent dough and center each triangle in a muffin cup, with the triangle points overhanging (once the filling is added, we will fold the points back in to encase it). Add 2 tablespoons of the cheesecake filling and 1 tablespoon lemon curd to each crescent roll.

3. Fold the crescent roll edges inward into the muffin cup's center and over the top of the filling.

4. Bake for 12 to 15 minutes, until the crescent rolls turn golden brown.

5. Let the rolls cool for 5 minutes, then sift powdered sugar over the top of each pastry and serve.

MAKE MEMORIES,

KEEP TRADITIONS,

AND CELEBRATE

EVERY DAY

Ice Cream Cookie Cups

There's nothing like chocolate chip cookies or vanilla ice cream . . . but pair the two, and you have a match made in dessert heaven! All you need to make this handheld treat is a package of cookie dough, a muffin tin, chocolate syrup, and your favorite vanilla ice cream. Just bake store-bought cookie dough in a muffin tin until golden brown, then press a greased shot glass into each warm cookie to create a cup. Fill each cookie cup with ice cream—enjoy!

Serves 12

Cooking spray

One 16-ounce tube refrigerated chocolate chip cookie dough (preferably Pillsbury)

12 scoops vanilla ice cream

Chocolate syrup

Sprinkles

1. Preheat the oven to 350°F. Grease 12 cups of a muffin tin with cooking spray.

2. Divide the cookie dough into 12 equal portions and place one portion in each muffin cup.

3. Bake for about 15 minutes, or until golden brown.

4. While the cookies are still warm, spray the outside of a shot glass with cooking spray and press it into each cookie to create a cup shape. Replenish the cooking spray on the shot glass every few cookies to prevent it from sticking.

5. Let cool for 20 minutes, then fill each cookie cup with a scoop of ice cream, a drizzle of chocolate syrup, and sprinkles. Serve immediately.

CELEBRATING TIP

For birthday parties, holidays, or everyday celebrations, add extra sprinkles that are customized to your favorite colors or are tied to the holiday you're celebrating.

Red, White, *and* Blue Angel Food Cake

Serves 8

1 store-bought angel food cake

One 8-ounce container Cool Whip or other whipped cream topping

1 cup sliced strawberries

1 cup blueberries

This store-bought shortcut is light and sweet for spring, summer parties, or even Fourth of July celebrations. Create a patriotic and fruity dessert with simple ingredients, including a store-bought angel food cake, fresh strawberries, blueberries, and Cool Whip. Growing up, I loved making angel food cake desserts with my mom, Mama Nancy. From adding homemade orange frosting to chocolate whipped topping, we'd have so much fun bumping angel food cakes up to the next level of deliciousness. Customize your angel food cake's frosting or whipped topping for any occasion by adding food coloring and sprinkles. Whether it's Valentine's Day or a birthday party, this shortcut will save you time and create happy memories.

1. Frost the cake with the Cool Whip using a spatula.

2. Decorate the top of the cake with the strawberries and blueberries.

Ice Cream Cupcake Cones

When I was growing up, Mama Nancy used to make these Ice Cream Cupcake Cones, and I thought she was an absolute genius! All you do is place ice cream cones in a muffin tin and bake cake batter in each cone. The frosting on top totally makes it look like ice cream. I can wholeheartedly say this is another childhood nostalgic dessert that inspired me at *Best Friends for Frosting*, and especially for this very book. It taught me firsthand the importance of investing time in childhood memories that would one day become happy, nostalgic, and warm. No one can take happy memories from us.

Serves 12

One 13.25-ounce box rainbow sprinkle cake mix

4 large egg whites, for the cake batter

½ cup vegetable oil, for the cake batter

12 flat-bottomed ice cream cones

One 16-ounce can vanilla frosting

Colorful sprinkles

12 maraschino cherries

1. Preheat the oven to 350°F.

2. Prepare the cake batter according to the package directions.

3. Place the cones in a 12-cup muffin tin and fill each cone two-thirds of the way up with batter. Be careful not to overfill as the batter will expand and overflow.

4. Bake for about 15 minutes, or until a toothpick inserted in the center of each cupcake comes out clean.

5. Let cool for 15 to 20 minutes. Frost the cooled cupcakes and decorate with sprinkles and a maraschino cherry.

Rainbow Sprinkle Cheesecake Cups

Makes 12 mini cheesecakes

1 cup graham cracker crumbs

4 tablespoons unsalted butter, melted

Two 8-ounce packages cream cheese, at room temperature

¾ cup sugar

1 teaspoon vanilla extract

2 large eggs

⅓ cup rainbow sprinkles

FOR SERVING

Whipped cream

Sprinkles

You know that friend who makes you laugh so hard you snort? The one you can't even make eye contact with during a serious event without cracking up? The one who can turn any trip to the grocery store into a hilarious adventure? That's my partner in crime Amy. From the moment we met in kindergarten at the snack table, dipping our graham crackers in milk together, we instantly clicked and have been best friends ever since. Our shared sense of humor sprinkled our friendship with constant laughter, and allowed us to find the funny in everyday life. Our teachers even had it in our school files that we were too much of a giggling disaster to be in the same class together.

Just as our friendship brightens even the darkest days, these delightful Rainbow Sprinkle Cheesecake Cups are a sweet way to celebrate and cherish those unforgettable moments with the ones we love most. A few people will change your life forever—go find them! Cheers to love, friendship, and the sweet moments that make life truly special!

1. Preheat the oven to 350°F. Line 12 cups of a muffin tin with cupcake liners.

2. In a small bowl, stir together the graham cracker crumbs and melted butter until combined. It should look like wet sand.

3. Add a heaping tablespoon of graham cracker crumbs to each muffin cup. Use the bottom of a measuring cup or spoon to press the crumbs firmly into the bottom of each cup.

4. Bake the crusts for 5 minutes, until they turn golden brown. Remove from the oven and let cool.

recipe continues

5. In a large bowl with an electric mixer, beat the cream cheese until smooth. Mix in the sugar and vanilla and continue to beat until combined. Beat in the eggs, one at a time. Fold in the rainbow sprinkles.

6. Fill each muffin cup with 2½ tablespoons of the cheesecake mixture.

7. Bake for 15 to 18 minutes, until the cheesecake sets.

8. Allow the mini cheesecakes to cool completely in the pan at room temperature.

9. Once cooled, gently remove from the muffin tin, place in an airtight container in the refrigerator and refrigerate for 2 to 3 hours before serving. Serve with a dollop of whipped cream and more sprinkles.

**Family recipes become
cherished nostalgic
reminders of the love and
joy that filled our homes**

FRUITY TREATS

Who would have known fruity treats could be SO much fun? With just a little imagination, you can easily transform simple fruits into festive treats to make any occasion feel extra special! You'll be whipping up White Chocolate Strawberry Heart Pops (page 136) and adorable Banana Ghosts and Orange Pumpkins (page 150) and Watermelon "Fries" with Strawberry Yogurt Dip (page 149) in no time at all—true story! So, what are you waiting for?! Bring on the holiday magic and seasonal surprises, and sprinkle a little everyday joy over the ones you love most.

White Chocolate Strawberry Heart Pops

Makes 20 pops

20 strawberries (about 2 pounds)

12 ounces (1½ cups) white candy melts

20 cake pop sticks

When I was growing up, Valentine's Day was one of my absolute favorite holidays! I loved everything about it—the cute cards, the sweet treats, the whole classroom filled with love. The sight of these White Chocolate Strawberry Heart Pops instantly brings back memories of Valentine's Day parties in my childhood classroom. And did I mention how easy they are to make? Cut notches into strawberries to create a heart shape, add a cake pop stick, dip them in white chocolate or candy melts, and set them on parchment paper to harden quickly, and you're all set. These strawberry pops are healthier than cake pops but taste just as sweet. You can even make them with milk chocolate. I love adding fruit to the menu for sweet celebrations, birthdays, and Valentine's Day alike.

1. With a paring knife, make two diagonal cuts on the top of each strawberry to remove the stem and create a heart shape.

2. In a microwave-safe bowl, microwave the white candy melts in 30-second intervals, stirring in between, until melted, about 1 minute total. Be careful not to overheat it as the chocolate may seize up.

3. Line a baking sheet with parchment paper. Insert a cake pop stick into the bottom of each strawberry and dip the top of the heart halfway into the melted chocolate. Place on the parchment paper and let set for 10 to 15 minutes.

Rainbow Fruit Board

The kid within me loves Saint Patrick's Day. I love the colors, the magic, and the tradition of making this rainbow fruit board. Another family tradition that fills my heart with joy is putting together "Lucky Buckets" for the kids, with all the green and rainbow goodies that make my heart happy—from green apples to lime yogurt to green Gatorade to even a green Xbox gift card. They're sort of like green-themed Easter baskets. Once the kids fall fast asleep, I turn the dining room into a party and carefully arrange the buckets. In the morning, everyone wakes up to a breakfast with Lucky Charms cereal, alongside green eggs and ham. And as the day rolls on, I prepare a cozy slow cooker dinner of corned beef and cabbage, and this fruit board. Saint Patrick's Day at our house is nothing short of a magical experience sprinkled with love, fun, and lucky surprises!

Serves 12

2½ cups strawberries, hulled and halved

6 Cuties clementines, separated into segments

1 cup canned pineapple chunks

½ cup green grapes

¼ cup blueberries

2 cups mini marshmallows

1. Arrange the strawberries, clementines, pineapple, grapes, and blueberries on the top half of an oval platter to resemble a rainbow.

2. Arrange the marshmallows to resemble clouds on the bottom of each side of the rainbow and serve immediately.

CELEBRATING TIP

To make this Rainbow Fruit Board extra festive, include a small dish of gold-wrapped candies, such as Rolos, as the pot of gold at the end of the rainbow.

Make happy memories this Saint Patrick's Day by starting your own Lucky Bucket tradition with adorable custom tags! Leap on over to **BestFriendsForFrosting.com/FreePrintables** *to download yours.*

Strawberry Jell-O Pretzel Salad

Serves 12

PRETZEL CRUST

2 cups crushed pretzels

8 tablespoons (1 stick) butter, melted

3 tablespoons sugar

FILLING

One 8-ounce package cream cheese, at room temperature

¾ cup sugar

One 8-ounce container Cool Whip, or other whipped cream topping

One 6-ounce box strawberry Jell-O

1½ cups boiling water

1 large red apple, cored and chopped

1 cup chopped walnuts

Over the past sixty years, my husband Andy's Grandma Arlene has perfected her family-favorite Strawberry Jell-O Pretzel Salad, originally shared by a friend in Nashville, Tennessee. It's a staple at our celebrations, from holidays and baby showers (including mine when I was pregnant with Charlie!) to church potlucks, where Arlene always makes two—one to share and one for the dedicated "kitchen help." It is one of our favorite desserts. The heavenly combination of sweet, salty, and fruity flavors takes it to the next level. It is pure perfection and one of my all-time favorite desserts—a guaranteed highlight at any of Andy's family gatherings.

1. Preheat the oven to 375°F.

2. Make the pretzel crust: In a medium bowl, stir together the crushed pretzels, melted butter, and sugar. Spread into an even layer in the bottom of a 9 × 13-inch baking dish.

3. Bake for about 8 minutes, or until the pretzel crust is a deep golden brown, especially around the edges. Let cool.

4. Make the filling: In a large bowl, with an electric mixer, mix the cream cheese and sugar until combined. Add the Cool Whip and mix just until evenly combined. Spread the mixture into an even layer over the pretzel crust and refrigerate for 30 minutes.

5. In a heatproof bowl, stir the Jell-O powder into the boiling water to dissolve. Then stir in 1½ cups cold water. Let cool in the refrigerator for about 1 hour, until the Jell-O is partially set.

6　Add the chopped apples and walnuts to the Jell-O. Pour the Jell-O mixture over the whipped cream cheese layer, cover with plastic wrap, and refrigerate. For the best texture and flavor, chill for at least 4 hours, but preferably overnight.

7　Just before serving, use a knife to cut the chilled salad into neat squares.

Watermelon Blueberry Fruit Sparklers

*Makes
20 skewers*

1 large seedless
watermelon

2 pints large blueberries

Twenty 12-inch wooden
skewers

This two-ingredient fruity treat is splendid for a hot summer day and especially for the Fourth of July. Hello, red, white, and blue! The skewers make it feel like you're holding a wand, taking it to a new level of fun for little ones.

1. Cut the watermelon into ¾-inch-thick slices.

2. Cut star shapes out of the watermelon slices using a small star cookie cutter.

3. Slide a watermelon star and 3 blueberries onto a skewer, leaving a few inches of space at the bottom for a handle. Alternate the watermelon and blueberry until you reach the top of the skewer.

> ### CELEBRATING TIP
>
> I learned the "decide once" method from Kendra Adachi of *The Lazy Genius*. It's a strategy to combat overwhelm and indecisiveness by making a one-time decision and sticking to it until it no longer serves you. If I could go back in time, I would tell myself to decide once and make these Watermelon Blueberry Fruit Sparklers my go-to handheld Fourth of July dessert every year. They're healthy, inexpensive, and oh-so-festive! What holiday dessert traditions can you decide once on that you will make each year as your go-to treat?

Starry Fruit Salad

After my dad had a stroke, one of his biggest wishes was to come home, be surrounded by family, and enjoy a refreshing fruit salad. As he lay in his hospital bed, he would recite all the different fruits he imagined in this special fruit salad for our family gathering. Now, whenever I see ANY fruit salad, it reminds me of the blessings of his recovery. This star-shaped fruit salad has become a joy, adding a bright, starry touch to our Fourth of July gatherings. It's a delicious and healthy way to celebrate the sweet moments that make life truly so special.

Serves 8

1 medium seedless watermelon

1 pint blueberries

2½ cups strawberries, hulled and halved

3 large Granny Smith apples, cored and peeled

1. Slice the watermelon into ¾-inch-thick slices. Use a medium star cookie cutter to cut out star shapes from the watermelon slices. Place the watermelon stars in a large serving bowl.

2. Add the blueberries and strawberries to the bowl with the watermelon stars and mix.

3. Slice the apples into ¾-inch-thick slices. Use a small star cookie cutter to cut out star shapes from the apple slices. Decoratively place the apple stars on top of the rest of the fruit salad and serve immediately.

Frozen Banana Pops

*Makes
8 pops*

4 firm bananas

8 cake pop sticks

16 ounces (2 cups) white candy melts

Sprinkles or chopped peanuts

These Frozen Banana Pops are incredibly easy to make, require only a few simple ingredients, and are guaranteed to put a smile on everyone's face! Get creative with the toppings and dip the bananas in white candy melts, crushed nuts, or colorful sprinkles. You can even drizzle peanut butter or honey over them for extra flavor.

1. Peel and cut each banana in half crosswise and insert a cake pop stick into the cut end of each banana half. Freeze for 3 hours or up to overnight.

2. In a microwave-safe bowl, microwave the white candy melts in 30-second intervals, stirring in between, until melted, about 1 minute total.

3. Line a baking sheet with parchment paper. Pour the melted chocolate into a tall cup to make it easier to dip the banana halves. Dip each banana into the chocolate and top with sprinkles or peanuts. Place on the parchment paper and let set for 15 to 20 minutes.

4. Serve immediately.

Watermelon "Fries" *with* Strawberry Yogurt Dip

Isn't it amazing how just changing the shape of a familiar fruit can make it SO much more exciting? I've always loved watermelon, but watermelon "fries" were a revelation—talk about love at first bite! I was inspired by Heather Staller of *Happy Kids Kitchen* when she took TikTok by storm with her watermelon fries, turning them into a social media craze! Now they've become one of our family's favorite summer treats! If you don't own a crinkle cutter (I found mine on Amazon for under $15), it's a game changer for healthy snacks. My kids, Charlie and Claire, love crinkle-cut cucumbers dipped in ranch and especially Apple Crinkle "Fries" with Cream Cheese Caramel Toffee Dip (page 154). But most of all, we love pairing these oh-so-refreshing watermelon fries with a creamy strawberry yogurt dip to make a perfect summer treat!

Serves 8

1 medium seedless watermelon

1 cup vanilla Greek yogurt

4 large strawberries, hulled

½ teaspoon lemon juice

1 tablespoon honey

1. Slice the watermelon into ¾-inch-thick slices. With a crinkle cutter, cut out fry shapes.

2. In a blender, blend together the Greek yogurt, strawberries, lemon juice, and honey.

3. Pour the yogurt dip into a serving dish. Place the dip in the middle of a round platter and arrange the watermelon fries around it.

Banana Ghosts *and* Orange Pumpkins

Serves 8

2 celery stalks

8 Cuties clementines, peeled

4 bananas

16 mini chocolate chips

Add a festive and healthy twist to your family's Halloween celebrations with this fab-boo-lous snack. I like to pack these in school lunches or serve as a fall after-school snack. These were a hit in my daughter Claire's classroom party. Who would have thought bananas with chocolate chip eyes could be so cute? And don't get me started on the Cuties pumpkins with celery stems. They're almost too cute to eat!

1. Use a paring knife to cut ½-inch-long pieces out of the celery to resemble pumpkin stems. Insert one into the top of each clementine.

2. Peel the bananas. Cut one-third off each end to make 2 ghosts (you'll end up with middle pieces that you can snack on). Insert 2 mini chocolate chips into each banana piece for the ghost's eyes.

Caramel Apple Cream Cheese Board

This Caramel Apple Cream Cheese Board is a sweet and crunchy crowd-pleaser! I love setting it out on the counter for afternoon snacking or for entertaining at the last minute. It's a burst of fall flavor with just a few simple ingredients: whipped cream cheese spread, caramel sauce, toffee candy bits, chopped peanuts, and tart Granny Smith apples, giving it a perfect sweet-and-tangy balance.

Serves 8

1. In a medium bowl, stir together the whipped cream cheese and 1 cup of the caramel sauce until combined.

2. Spread the mixture evenly in the center of a round cutting board or plate. Drizzle with the remaining ½ cup caramel sauce and sprinkle with the toffee bits and chopped peanuts.

3. Arrange the apple slices around the cream cheese and serve immediately.

One 16-ounce container whipped cream cheese spread

1½ cup caramel sauce

6 tablespoons toffee candy bits

6 tablespoons chopped peanuts

5 Granny Smith apples, cored and sliced

Apple Crinkle "Fries" *with* Cream Cheese Caramel Toffee Dip

Serves 6

These crispy and crunchy apple crinkle "fries" paired with cream cheese caramel toffee dip will take your fruit-eating experience to a whole new level of fun. Not only are they decadent for snacking, but they even make an enjoyable addition to any lunchbox. So grab a handful of these fruity fries and let the crunching and dipping fun begin!

6 Granny Smith apples

One 8-ounce package cream cheese, at room temperature

1 cup caramel sauce, plus more for serving

¼ cup toffee bits, plus more for serving

1. Cut the apples into wedges and trim off the tough core (I like using an apple slicer). Use a crinkle cutter to cut the apple slices into crinkle fries.

2. In a medium bowl, with an electric mixer, beat the cream cheese and caramel sauce together. Fold in the toffee bits.

3. Transfer the dip to a small round dish, drizzle with additional caramel sauce, and garnish with more toffee bits.

4. Place the dip in the center of a serving plate and arrange the apple fries around it. Serve immediately.

Chocolate-Dipped Strawberry Reindeer

I may have believed in Santa a bit too long. When I was ten, I even left him a note asking for a ride on his sleigh with the reindeer—I was convinced it would work! Maybe these cute reindeer strawberries would have done the trick?! Transform ordinary strawberries into adorable Rudolphs with just a few ingredients, creativity, and holiday magic. They're easy and guaranteed to disappear faster than Santa sneaking down the chimney. These cheerful treats will surely bring a smile to everyone's face, whether young or old or just a kid at heart (like me).

Serves 12

16 ounces (2 cups) chocolate candy melts

24 strawberries

48 candy eyeballs

24 red M&M's

1 cup pretzels

1. In a large microwave-safe bowl, microwave the chocolate candy melts in 30-second intervals, stirring in between, until melted, about 1 minute total.

2. Line a baking sheet with parchment paper. Dip the strawberries in the melted chocolate and place on the parchment paper. Immediately after dipping each strawberry, place 2 candy eyeballs and a red M&M nose in the chocolate to create a reindeer face.

3. Break the pretzels into pieces. Insert 2 pretzel pieces into the top of each strawberry to resemble antlers and serve immediately.

**DON'T LET YOUR ICE
CREAM MELT WHILE
COUNTING SOMEBODY
ELSE'S SPRINKLES**

Orange Jell-O Salad

My middle name is Ann, after my mom's sister, Jo Ann. Back in the day, long before the internet, my Aunt Jo Ann wrote a cookbook called *What's Cooking in Oregon*. I always tease her and tell her she would have been the best recipe influencer out there if blogs were a thing in her day. One of her famous, well-known recipes has always been her Orange Jell-O Salad. All throughout my childhood and adult years, my mom has made this recipe for every single holiday—the Fourth of July, Easter, Christmas, and even Thanksgiving. We could depend on the fact that this salad would be on the table, almost always displayed in a clear glass bowl. In my late teens, I got in trouble for sneaking into my mom's Orange Jell-O Salad before it was set. Let's just say I left a noticeable dent (and had a bit of a guilty conscience, too).

Mixing Cool Whip, cottage cheese, fruit, and Jell-O together might sound wild, but these flavors are like a supergroup when combined—even people who don't like cottage cheese end up loving this recipe. Heck, I'm not even a cottage cheese fan, but I LOVE this recipe.

Serves 6

One 16-ounce container cottage cheese

One 8-ounce container extra-creamy Cool Whip

One 3-ounce box orange Jell-O

One 8-ounce can pineapple chunks

One 15-ounce can mandarin oranges

1. In a large bowl, mix together the cottage cheese and Cool Whip. Gently fold in the orange Jell-O powder until well combined.

2. Drain the pineapple and mandarin oranges well, then pat them dry with paper towels. Gently fold the pineapple and oranges into the cottage cheese mixture.

3. Refrigerate the Jell-O salad, covered with plastic wrap, for at least 3 hours or overnight for the best results, to allow the flavors to meld.

4. The salad will begin to soften at room temperature, so plan to serve within 20 to 30 minutes of removing it from the refrigerator. For easy serving, use an ice cream scoop to portion.

STORAGE

Store in an airtight container in the refrigerator for up to 3 days.

CHOCOLATE CELEBRATIONS

Chocolate isn't just a dessert, it's a total party starter! In this chapter, we're celebrating all the ways chocolate can turn any occasion into something truly special. From birthdays to holidays to happy Mondays (yes, I totally love Mondays!), get ready to take your daily celebrations to a whole new level of happy with these delicious chocolate recipes.

This "Chocolate Celebrations" chapter is filled to the brim with all kinds of surprises! I'm finally sharing our Family-Favorite Fudge Birthday Cake (page 163)—a recipe I was sworn to secrecy to save for my first cookbook. Plus, there's the recipe for the gooey Grilled Chocolate and Marshmallow Sandwich (page 165) I stashed away for my (now-chocolate-loving!) kids when I was just twenty years young. And I can hardly wait for you to try our viral Christmas Saltine Cracker Toffee (page 173)—it's a *Best Friends for Frosting* fan favorite! Consider the chocolate recipes in this chapter a sweet reminder that there are rich moments of sweetness and joy sprinkled ahead.

Family-Favorite Fudge Birthday Cake

When I started *Best Friends for Frosting* in 2011, I promised myself I would only share my husband Andy's Grandma Arlene's chocolate cake recipe once I had my own cookbook. Fourteen years later, and it's finally here! Arlene got the recipe from a friend in South Dakota back in 1964, and it quickly became a beloved family birthday tradition.

I have indulged in numerous chocolate cakes, but none have come close to the one we have for Andy's birthday every year. This cake is pure heaven—moist, decadent chocolate paired with a luscious fudge frosting that melts in your mouth. This recipe has a little secret—shortening! It gives the cake an incredibly light, fluffy texture and keeps it extra moist. It's truly the best chocolate cake recipe out there.

1. Preheat the oven to 350°F. Grease a 9 × 13-inch cake pan with shortening. Dust the greased pan with all-purpose flour, tapping gently to remove any excess.

2. In a large bowl, combine the shortening, brown sugar, and granulated sugar and mix until evenly combined. Stir in the cocoa powder, eggs, vanilla, and salt. Once the mixture is uniform, add the flour and buttermilk and mix until combined.

3. In a small heatproof bowl, stir the baking soda into the boiling water to dissolve. Pour the baking soda mixture into the batter and mix until evenly combined. Pour the batter into the greased and floured pan and even it out.

4. Bake for 35 minutes, or until a toothpick inserted into the center comes out clean. Set aside and let cool.

recipe continues

1 cup shortening (I like Crisco), plus more for greasing the pan

2 cups all-purpose flour, plus more for dusting the pan

1 cup packed light brown sugar

1 cup granulated sugar

½ cup unsweetened cocoa powder

2 large eggs

1 teaspoon vanilla extract

½ teaspoon salt

½ cup buttermilk

1 teaspoon baking soda

1 cup boiling water

FROSTING

2 cups granulated sugar

½ cup unsweetened cocoa powder

8 tablespoons (1 stick) margarine

½ cup milk

1 teaspoon vanilla extract

Sprinkles

5. Meanwhile, make the frosting: In a medium saucepan, combine the granulated sugar, cocoa powder, margarine, and milk and bring to a boil over medium heat. Boil vigorously for 2 minutes, stirring frequently. Remove from the heat and let the frosting cool for 5 minutes. Stir in the vanilla and beat until the frosting starts to thicken.

6. Spread the frosting evenly over the chocolate cake, add the sprinkles, and let the cake cool at room temperature for 1 hour to allow the frosting to set before serving.

CELEBRATING TIP

Create lasting birthday memories by using a special cake server or plate to serve your cake on each year. My mother-in-law started this tradition years ago with the prettiest cake server decorated with bright colors and polka dots, and it's become such a special family tradition. And can you guess which superstar cake we've used our cake slicer on the most? You guessed it! Our Family-Favorite Fudge Birthday Cake.

Grilled Chocolate *and* Marshmallow Sandwich

As a twenty-year-old on a budget, I loved this recipe because I already had all the ingredients on hand—bread, butter, chocolate chips, and marshmallow crème. And the verdict?! It was amazing! The combination of melted chocolate and marshmallow crème, sandwiched between two slices of crispy grilled buttered bread, was too good to forget. I even remember thinking how much fun making this treat for my future kids would be. I was right—I knew they would be just as excited as I was to discover a dessert sandwich.

1. Heat a small skillet over medium heat.

2. Spread each slice of bread with marshmallow crème and top one slice with the chocolate chips. Sandwich the slices together.

3. Butter each side of the sandwich.

4. Cook until golden brown, about 3 minutes per side.

*Makes
1 sandwich*

2 slices white bread

2 tablespoons marshmallow crème

3 tablespoons chocolate chips

1 tablespoon butter, at room temperature

Sundae Bar

Serves 8

Get ready to cool down on hot summer days and celebrate with a Sundae Bar! This easy idea has become one of my absolute favorites, as the kids always get excited about creating their customized sundaes. The best part? It only takes minutes to set up! I prep everything in advance by adding all the toppings to muffin cups and covering with plastic wrap to store. And I pre-portion the ice cream in fun cupcake liners and pop those in the freezer, too. Add a variety of toppings, colorful spoons, and party plates, and you'll have a simple yet impressive setup that will make you feel like the ultimate party planner.

TOPPINGS

½ cup maraschino cherries

½ cup blueberries

½ cup chopped strawberries

½ cup white chocolate chips

½ cup chocolate chips

½ cup rainbow sprinkles

½ cup pastel sprinkles

½ cup chocolate sprinkles

½ cup chopped nuts

½ cup shredded coconut

½ cup M&M's

½ cup mini marshmallows

FOR SERVING

Ice cream

Chocolate syrup

Caramel syrup

Whipped cream

1. Fill 12 cups of a muffin tin with the toppings, one topping per cup, to create an easy serving platter.

2. Serve with ice cream, syrups, and whipped cream.

S'Mores Treats

When I was growing up, my parents always let my brothers and all our friends roast marshmallows after we had outdoor barbecued dinners. I remember one year my marshmallow even caught on fire. I nearly flung it across the backyard trying to get the flame to blow out. These s'mores treats were practically made for daredevils like me—*wink!* No baking or roasting required. This is an easy way to combine all the classic flavors of s'mores into a quick, no-bake dessert—no campfire required!

Serves 9

7 cups Golden Grahams cereal

One 16-ounce bag mini marshmallows

¾ cup milk chocolate chips

7 tablespoons salted butter, melted

Cooking spray

6 snack-size milk chocolate bars, chopped

1. In a large bowl, gently fold together the cereal, 2 cups of the marshmallows, and the chocolate chips until evenly mixed and set aside.

2. In a microwave-safe medium bowl, add the remaining marshmallows, reserving a handful for topping later. Add the melted butter to the bowl and microwave in 30-second intervals, stirring well, until the marshmallows are fully melted and the mixture is smooth and glossy, about 1 minute total.

3. Add the cereal mixture to the melted marshmallow/butter mixture and fold in until combined.

4. Line a 9 × 13-inch baking dish with parchment paper, leaving a few inches of excess around the edges. Grease the parchment with cooking spray.

5. Spread the cereal/marshmallow mixture in an even layer in the dish. Press the reserved marshmallows and chopped chocolate bars on top and refrigerate until set, 30 to 45 minutes.

6. Remove the treats from the baking dish using the excess parchment paper as a handle. Slice into squares and serve.

STORAGE

Store in an airtight container at room temperature for up to 5 days.

Fall Harvest Mix

Serves 8

5 cups Rice Chex cereal

5 cups Corn Chex cereal

4 cups pretzels

One 7-ounce bag Bugles

1½ sticks (6 ounces) unsalted butter, melted

¾ cup packed light brown sugar

1 tablespoon vanilla extract

1 cup candy corn

1 cup candy corn pumpkins

One 8-ounce bag Reese's Pieces

Just like Charlie Brown waits for the Great Pumpkin, my kids and I watch *It's the Great Pumpkin, Charlie Brown* every single year. It has become a beloved tradition we look forward to, and it brings back so many happy memories from my own childhood. This Fall Harvest Mix captures that same nostalgic feeling—it's the perfect treat for a cozy night in, reliving the magic of the season. This is the best combination of sweet, salty, and crunchy for fall, Halloween, and, better yet, a family movie night. It's made with Chex cereal, Bugles, pretzels, and nostalgic seasonal candies like candy corn, candy corn pumpkins, and Reese's Pieces, with a brown sugar butter drizzle as the star of the show.

1. Preheat the oven to 275°F. Line a large baking sheet with parchment paper.

2. In a large bowl, mix together the cereals, pretzels, and Bugles.

3. In a small bowl, stir together the melted butter, brown sugar, and vanilla until combined. Pour the brown sugar butter mixture over the cereal mix and toss until evenly coated. Spread the mixture evenly onto the lined baking sheet.

4. Bake until golden brown, about 30 minutes.

5. Let cool, then sprinkle on the candy corn, candy pumpkins, and Reese's Pieces.

From pumpkin patches to cozy movie nights, create a memorable fall with your loved ones using my FREE printable bucket list. Available at **BestFriendsForFrosting.com/FreePrintables.**

Christmas Saltine Cracker Toffee

This Christmas Saltine Cracker Toffee recipe is an all-time favorite in our house! It's all about marrying sweet and salty together. Imagine a tray of saltine crackers covered in a luscious layer of toffee, with a rich, melted chocolate spread on top and festive sprinkles for extra cheer. It's not only incredibly easy to make, but it's also seriously addictive. My kids and their friends go wild over it! I've heard the same from followers at *Best Friends for Frosting*—it takes them right back to their own happy childhood memories. These are especially a hit to gift in a cute tin for the holidays.

Serves 12

48 saltine crackers

2 sticks (8 ounces) butter, melted

1 cup packed light brown sugar

One 12-ounce bag chocolate chips

Christmas sprinkles

1. Preheat the oven to 350°F. Line a large baking sheet with parchment paper.

2. Arrange the crackers on the lined baking sheet into a rectangle, ensuring all the crackers touch each other.

3. In a small saucepan, melt the butter and brown sugar. Bring to a boil and stir frequently for 2 to 3 minutes. Pour over the crackers and spread evenly with a spatula.

4. Sprinkle the chocolate chips evenly over the top of the crackers and transfer to the oven.

5. Bake until the chocolate chips are melted, about 5 minutes.

6. Using a spatula, evenly spread the melted chocolate chips into an even layer over the crackers. Add the Christmas sprinkles to the top of the melted chocolate.

7. Refrigerate for 2 hours. Flip the crackers over, remove the parchment paper from the back, and gently break into bite-size pieces.

> **CELEBRATING TIP**
>
> **Don't have any saltine crackers on hand?** *Best Friends for Frosting* **followers have shared that replacing the saltine crackers with graham crackers is also a hit!**

Chocolate-Covered Peanut Butter Balls

Serves 8

1 stick (4 ounces) butter, melted

2¼ cups crunchy peanut butter

3¾ cups powdered sugar

3 cups Rice Krispies cereal

32 ounces (4 cups) chocolate candy melts

Talk about an irresistible treat! When I joined my husband Andy's family, I was blown away by my mother-in-law Barbara's cookie-making skills, especially at Christmas. She was like a baking machine, busting out hundreds of homemade cookies. Out of all the cookies she has made, Andy's all-time favorite has always been her Chocolate-Covered Peanut Butter Balls. These bite-size treats are a touchdown of flavor with a rich chocolate coating and irresistible peanut butter filling.

1. In a large bowl, mix together the melted butter, peanut butter, and powdered sugar. Fold in the Rice Krispies until well combined.

2. Form into small bite-size balls, then freeze for 30 minutes to 1 hour.

3. In a medium microwave-safe bowl or cup, microwave the chocolate candy melts in 30-second intervals, stirring in between, until melted, about 1 minute total.

4. Line a baking sheet with parchment paper. Insert a toothpick into each ball, dip it into the chocolate until covered, and place it on the parchment paper. Cool in the freezer for 30 minutes, then remove the toothpicks.

CELEBRATING TIP

Snowball fights are so yesterday . . . Start a food fight with these perfectly round chocolate-covered peanut butter balls. Just kidding! I just wanted to shock whoever was reading this.

Chocolate Peanut Butter Energy Balls

When I was growing up, Reese's Peanut Butter Cups were my all-time favorite candy. I consider these Chocolate Peanut Butter Energy Balls a healthier and even more fulfilling version of the nostalgic childhood candy (that I still enjoy). Packed with pantry staple ingredients like peanut butter, chocolate chips, rolled oats, and honey, these bite-size treats boost energy and satisfy sweet tooths, making them perfect for an after-school snack or lunchbox addition.

1. In a large bowl, mix together the oats, chocolate chips, peanut butter, and honey until combined. Roll into bite-size balls.

2. If serving the same day, freeze for 1 hour to ensure the energy balls firm up enough for easy handling. Thaw at room temperature for 10 minutes before serving.

Serves 6

2 cups rolled oats

1 cup chocolate chips

1 cup crunchy peanut butter

⅔ cup honey

STORAGE

Freeze in an airtight container for up to 2 months to maintain best taste and texture. Thaw for 10 minutes before serving.

HOLIDAY CHEER ALL YEAR

Get ready to sprinkle a little holiday magic into every season! From the joyful festivities of Christmas to the love-filled moments of Valentine's Day, from the warmth of Thanksgiving to the spooky fun of Halloween, and all the special occasions in between, this chapter is filled with thoughtful ideas to create happy food memories leading up to each holiday all year long.

As the seasons change, so does the festive food fun! Whether you want to whip up a quick Valentine Snack Mix (page 180), transform pretzels into Saint Patrick's Day shamrocks (see page 183), or craft adorable bunnies out of refrigerated cinnamon roll dough (see page 184), these recipes are truly just as easy as they are memorable.

As you read through these food memory ideas—which can be lovingly prepared to help you celebrate your happiest occasions all year—I am cheering for you to use them to create your own happy family memories that will last a lifetime. The days are long, but the years are short.

Unlock holiday cheer with my FREE printable holiday food memory planner. Available at **BestFriendsForFrosting.com/FreePrintables.**

Valentine Snack Mix

Serves 8

5 cups Corn Chex cereal

5 cups Rice Chex cereal

2 cups mini pretzel twists

24 ounces (3 cups) white candy melts

½ cup powdered sugar

1 cup Valentine's M&M's, plus more for serving

Valentine's sprinkles, for serving

Celebrate Valentine's Day with a sweet and festive snack mix made with Chex! This happy treat can be enjoyed in treat cups or served in colorful cupcake liners with pink, heart, or gingham patterns—festive for adding a touch of Valentine's Day charm to your snack table. So, gather your ingredients, mix it all, and sprinkle happy family memories with the sweetest snack to make your Valentine's Day even more special!

1. In a large bowl, mix together both cereals and the pretzels until combined.

2. Line a large baking sheet with parchment paper and spread the cereal mixture into an even layer.

3. In a microwave-safe bowl, microwave the white candy melts in 30-second intervals, stirring in between, until melted, about 1 minute total.

4. Measure out ¼ cup of the melted candy melts and set aside for finishing. Evenly drizzle the remaining melted candy melts over the cereal mixture and mix gently to combine, being careful not to crush the cereal. Immediately add the M&M's, then toss with the powdered sugar.

5. Let the cereal mixture cool until the white chocolate hardens, 10 to 15 minutes. Transfer to a large serving bowl.

6. Reheat the reserved ¼ cup candy melts and drizzle with a spoon over the mixture. Immediately top with additional M&M's and some sprinkles.

Pretzel Shamrocks

Sprinkle a little luck and a whole lot of smiles with these Pretzel Shamrocks! The first time I made these, my kids, Charlie and Claire, couldn't believe I was able to pull off making shamrocks out of such simple ingredients that we already had in our pantry. The mini pretzel twists become perfectly shaped shamrock leaves, a pretzel stick adds a whimsical stem, and a Rolo and M&M create a sweet, melt-in-your-mouth center that also holds everything together. They're the perfect mix of sweet, salty, memorable, and fun. It's like snack-time magic!

Makes 20 shamrocks

60 mini pretzel twists (about 7 cups)

20 pretzel sticks

20 Rolo chocolate caramels, unwrapped

20 green M&M's

1. Preheat the oven to 250°F. Line a baking sheet with parchment paper.

2. Arrange 3 mini pretzel twists around a pretzel stick on the baking sheet, ensuring that the round side of the twists faces inward. Repeat this to make 20 "shamrocks."

3. Place a Rolo in the middle of each shamrock and carefully put the baking sheet into the oven, without disturbing the shamrocks.

4. Bake the shamrocks for 2 minutes and remove from the oven.

5. Place 1 green M&M in the center of each Rolo and gently press down so that the softened Rolo flattens and touches each pretzel piece. Rearrange any pretzel pieces that may have become displaced.

6. Place the baking sheet in the refrigerator for 20 minutes for the Rolos to harden and set.

7. Remove from the refrigerator and carefully lift each shamrock off the parchment paper and arrange on a serving tray.

Bunny Cinnamon Rolls

*Makes
10 bunnies*

These three-ingredient cinna–bunnies are the cutest to kick off an Easter breakfast tradition or for a sunny spring morning. With just a can of cinnamon rolls, pastel M&M's, and sprinkles, you can create a fun and enjoyable treat that every bunny will love. Bake the cinnamon rolls, drizzle on the icing from the package, and top with M&M's and sprinkles for a festive touch.

Two 17.5-ounce cans
Pillsbury Grands!
Cinnamon Rolls with Icing

20 white M&M's

10 pink M&M's

Pastel sprinkles

1. Preheat the oven to 350°F. Line a baking sheet with parchment paper.

2. Unroll enough dough from the outer edge of each cinnamon roll to create the bunny ears. Loop the dough to form the left ear first and then the right ear. Press the end of the dough back into the cinnamon roll. Place the cinnamon rolls 1 to 2 inches apart on the lined baking sheet.

3. Bake for about 15 minutes, or until the cinnamon rolls are golden brown. If the cinnamon rolls are misshapen during baking, remove them from the oven and use a spoon to reshape them into a bunny shape, then continue baking.

4. Warm the packaged icing in the microwave for 15 seconds, then drizzle over the bunnies. Add white M&M's for the eyes and pink M&M's for the noses and top with the sprinkles.

Make Easter morning extra special with my FREE printable letter from the Easter Bunny. Hop on over to **BestFriendsForFrosting.com/FreePrintables** *to download yours.*

Easter Bunny Pudding Cups

Hop into the Easter spirit—you only need pudding cups, green shredded coconut, Peeps, and candy Easter eggs. These cuties are easy enough to batch-prep for a classroom party or even to let the kids get creative and make their own. We made these at my daughter Claire's first-grade classroom party, and the kids had an absolute ball customizing their cups with their favorite-colored bunnies and candies.

Serves 8

1. Add the coconut and 5 to 10 drops of green food coloring to a zip-top bag and shake until the coconut turns green.

2. Add a Peeps bunny to each pudding cup and arrange the shredded coconut around it to resemble grass.

3. Add 2 candy eggs at the base of each bunny.

1½ cups sweetened coconut

Green food coloring

8 Peeps bunnies

8 individual chocolate pudding cups

16 candy eggs

Bunny Butt Dip

Serves 8

1 cup rainbow sprinkle cake mix

Two 8-ounce packages cream cheese, at room temperature

1 cup white chocolate chips

¼ cup sugar

¾ cup rainbow sprinkles

One 14-ounce bag sweetened coconut flakes

8 pink M&M's

Graham crackers, for serving

One of my favorite Easter traditions with my mom is making a homemade bunny cake together. You know the one! It was so popular in magazines that my mom still has the photo she clipped in her album to this day. We'd add coconut flakes for fur, licorice for whiskers, and jelly beans for the eyes. I looked forward to making that cake every Easter, and little did I know that this sweet family memory would one day direct my professional life, leading me to help others celebrate their families and loved ones by making new food memories of their own.

Like mother, like daughter! I was inspired by the blog *Emily Enchanted* to create this new tradition, and now it's a family favorite. If you're looking for a whimsical dessert that captures the joy of Easter, look no further! This playful cookie dip combines the sweetness of rainbow sprinkle cake mix with the creaminess of cream cheese, resulting in a showstopping Easter treat that everyone will love and adore! It's so easy to make, and it's sure to be a hit at your next Easter gathering.

1. Preheat the oven to 350°F.

2. Spread the rainbow sprinkle cake mix on a baking sheet and bake for 5 minutes, or microwave in a small microwave-safe bowl in 30-second intervals, stirring in between, until the cake mix reaches 160°F (to ensure it's safe to eat). Let cool completely.

3. In a large bowl, mix together the cream cheese, white chocolate chips, sugar, sprinkles, and baked rainbow sprinkle cake mix.

4. Knead the mixture with your hands until everything is thoroughly combined.

5. Divide the mixture into 1 large ball (for the body), 2 medium-size balls (for the feet), and 1 small ball (for the tail).

recipe continues

6. To prevent the mixture from sticking, wet your hands before gently rolling each ball in the coconut flakes until completely coated.

7. Assemble the bunny butt on a serving platter by placing the large ball in the center, with the 2 medium-size balls (feet) slightly apart and the small ball (tail) above them.

8. Gently flatten and shape the feet with your hands.

9. Use the pink M&M's to create toes on the feet.

10. Refrigerate for at least 3 hours, or until firm, before serving.

11. Serve with graham crackers for dipping. Enjoy!

TIME IS THE BEST

GIFT YOU CAN

GIVE SOMEONE

Fourth of July Pretzels

Get ready to celebrate the Fourth of July with these flag pretzels! You know you're "extra" when you take mini pretzels and glam them into the cutest flags ever! With just a few simple ingredients, you can transform ordinary mini pretzels into a memorable holiday dessert that will look stunning displayed on a white dish served on the counter. These patriotic treats will be an absolute hit, making them the whimsical addition to your Fourth of July celebration!

Serves 6

4 ounces (½ cup) white candy melts

3 cups pretzel twists

4 ounces (½ cup) red candy melts

4 ounces (½ cup) blue candy melts

2 tablespoons star sprinkles

1. In a microwave-safe bowl, microwave the white candy melts in 30-second intervals, stirring in between, until melted, about 1 minute total.

2. Line a baking sheet with parchment paper. Dip the mini pretzels in the melted white chocolate and set on the parchment paper. Let cool at room temperature for 10 minutes to allow the melts to set up.

3. In another microwave-safe bowl, microwave the red candy melts in 30-second intervals, stirring in between, until melted, about 1 minute total. Using a spoon, drizzle the red candy melts over the pretzels to create a red-and-white-stripes effect. Let cool at room temperature for 10 minutes to allow the melts to set up.

4. In a third microwave-safe bowl, microwave the blue candy melts in 30-second intervals, stirring in between, until melted, about 1 minute total. Dip one-third of each pretzel into the blue candy melts and immediately add the white star sprinkles. Let cool at room temperature for 10 minutes to allow the melts to set up. Serve.

*Add extra sparkle to your Fourth of July with a fun and festive FREE printable treat tag. Available at **BestFriendsForFrosting.com/FreePrintables**.*

Back-to-School
Vanilla Wafer Pencils

12 vanilla wafers

⅓ cup white candy melts

12 mini chocolate chips

⅓ cup pink candy melts

CELEBRATING TIP

Kick off on the right foot and be the cheerleader to support your family by throwing a goodbye-summer party the day before back to school or making a first-day-of-school-celebration tradition.

Celebrating back to school truly sets the tone and can change an entire outlook. Start the brand-new school year fresh with these adorable pencil-shaped vanilla wafer cookies. Whether you're cheering on your child during their first month of school or want to sprinkle back-to-school joy like confetti, these treats are the celebrational way to show your support and make their day extra special.

1. Cut off the edges of one side of each vanilla wafer to create a triangular "pencil tip." Cut off the point of each wafer pencil tip. This will ensure a flat surface for the mini chocolate chip to adhere to.

2. Line a baking sheet with parchment paper. In a microwave-safe bowl, microwave the white candy melts in 30-second intervals, stirring in between, until melted, about 1 minute total. Dip each pencil tip into the melted white candy melts, then place a mini chocolate chip on the end to resemble the pencil lead. Place on the parchment and let cool for 5 minutes to allow the melts to set.

3. In another microwave-safe bowl, microwave the pink candy melts in 30-second intervals, stirring in between, until melted, about 1 minute total. Dip the opposite end of the vanilla wafers into the melted pink candy melts to create the erasers. Let cool at room temperature for 10 minutes to allow the melts to set up.

Celebrate the start of a new school year (and every day after!) with a cute FREE printable lunch note. Available at **BestFriendsForFrosting.com/FreePrintables.**

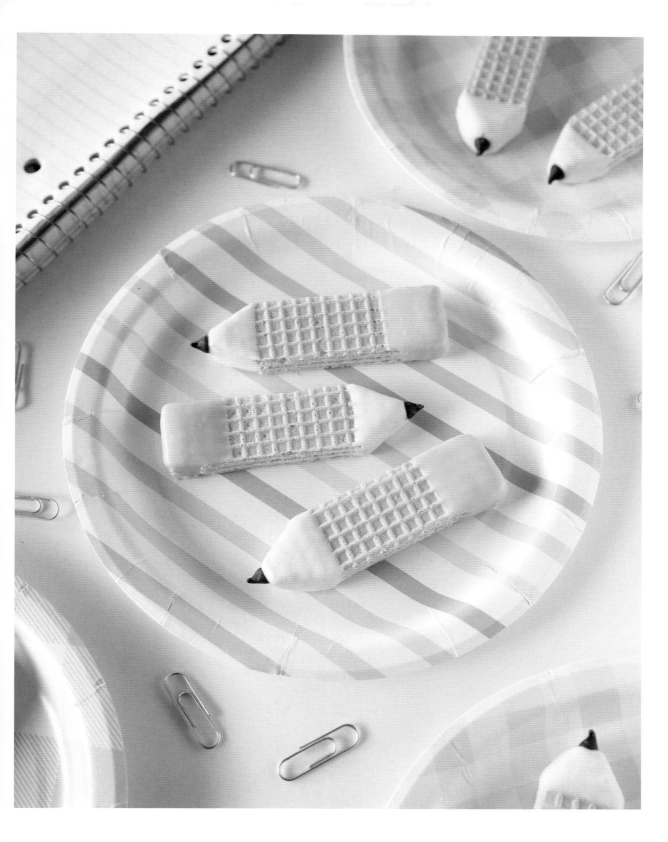

Back-to-School Mini Pretzel Apples

Makes
36 pretzel
apples

Back to school has always been my favorite time of the year. As fall welcomes us with crisp, cool air and leaves begin to change colors, it reminds us that change is remarkable. My mom would take me to Target every year to pick out my favorite school supplies. From glittery and flowy gel pens to decorative Lisa Frank folders to the most perfect hot pink JanSport backpack—back to school always felt like a holiday. Little did I know, my mom was setting the stage for a brand-new school year.

The apple doesn't fall far from the tree! I love celebrating the start of each new school year with my kids! We always kick it off with a fun celebration, including themed treats like the Back-to-School Vanilla Wafer Pencils (page 194). You can find colored fondant at grocery stores, making these pretzel apples easy to put together.

Cornstarch, for dusting

Green fondant

Brown fondant

10 ounces (1¼ cups) red candy melts

36 mini pretzels

1. To prepare the fondant decorations, lightly dust the countertop with cornstarch and then roll out each color of fondant until ⅛ inch thick. Using a paring knife, cut out 36 small leaf shapes from the green fondant and 36 apple stems from the brown fondant.

2. In a microwave-safe bowl, microwave the red candy melts in 30-second intervals, stirring in between, until melted.

3. Line a baking sheet with parchment paper. Dip each pretzel entirely into the red candy melts, let the excess drip off, and place on the parchment paper. Place a fondant leaf and stem on each pretzel immediately, while the candy melt is still warm. Let cool for 30 minutes to set.

Sprinkle excitement on the night before the first day of school! Download our FREE confetti printable and start a new tradition. Available at **BestFriendsForFrosting.com/FreePrintables.**

Graveyard Pudding Cups

Makes 8 pudding cups

10 Oreos

8 Peeps ghosts

8 individual chocolate pudding cups

8 candy corn pumpkins

Chocolate pudding, candy corn pumpkins, Oreos, and Peeps ghosts—oh my! These boo-fully sweet, not spooky, four-ingredient desserts will surely be a hit as you celebrate Halloween! Boo-lieve it or not, I have been making these no-bake Graveyard Pudding Cups with my oldest, Charlie, since he was in preschool! At the time, I had no idea it would become one of my most cherished memories in the kitchen. Fast-forward twelve years, and these memories feel nostalgic.

1. Place the Oreos in a zip-top bag and seal. Crush the Oreos with a rolling pin to make crumbs.

2. Add a Peeps ghost to each pudding cup and arrange the Oreo crumbs around them.

3. Place a candy pumpkin at the base of each ghost.

CELEBRATING TIP

Pick one easy childhood recipe to make each year for lasting memories. Think about other simple recipes you can make that can later become cherished memories. Add a reminder to your digital calendar and select the "event" to repeat each year. When Charlie was only three years old, I never imagined blinking and him suddenly being fourteen! To this day, Charlie is just as excited when we repeat this meaningful Halloween food tradition.

Powdered Donut Eyeballs

Get ready to make some spooktacular Halloween treats with this super-easy three-ingredient shortcut! You only need gummies, powdered donuts, and M&M's to create these festive treats. By pressing the gummy down on the donut, you will produce a cracked effect that makes it look like bloodshot eyes. These treats are always such a hit with the kids!

Makes
12 eyeballs

1. Stretch a Life Savers Gummy around each brown M&M.

2. Place a gummy on top of each powdered donut and lightly press down to embed the gummy into the donut.

12 Life Savers Gummies
12 brown M&M's
12 mini powdered donuts

Peanut Butter Cup Spider Cookies

Makes 12 spider cookies

Ready for the trick for your treat? Place a Reese's Peanut Butter Cup Mini on top of a cookie, add a couple of candy eyes, and pipe some chocolate frosting for the adorable spider legs.

¼ cup chocolate frosting

12 peanut butter cookies, store-bought or homemade

12 Reese's Peanut Butter Cup Minis

24 candy eyes

1. Add the chocolate frosting to a piping bag and pipe just a dab onto the center of each cookie. Set a peanut butter cup on top, wide side down.

2. Use the chocolate frosting to pipe 3 legs coming out of each side of the peanut butter cup spider.

3. Attach 2 candy eyes to the top of each peanut butter cup with the remaining chocolate frosting.

CELEBRATING TIP

You don't have to spend time in the kitchen to make memories! Starting happy food traditions can be as simple as letting your favorite coffee shop, restaurant, or bakery be the secret ingredient in your next family tradition.

Even when I was a little girl, each year for Valentine's Day, my mom would get red heart-shaped frosted sugar cookies from our neighborhood bakery, Freeport Bakery, for my brother and me. And now, like clockwork each year, I take the kids to McDonald's in March to get a Shamrock Shake for Saint Patrick's Day. And when Easter candy pops up in stores, I'm always hunting for those chocolate-covered marshmallow egg candies for my dad. It's basically the first day of fall in my book when Starbucks releases Pumpkin Spice everything—whether the calendar agrees or not! And finally, every Christmas, my mom and I get our first red cup from Starbucks together, along with a Cranberry Bliss Bar (of course).

Building happy food traditions doesn't have to be complicated—the simple joy of excitement, anticipation, and togetherness is what truly makes these traditions special.

What delicious traditions can you create with your family to look forward to each year?

Donut Spiders

Imagine the smiles, the giggles, the sticky fingers . . . and, years later, the warm memories of Halloween fun. These adorable and oh-so-easy donut spiders are a not-too-spooky Halloween treat that will create those sweet, nostalgic moments. With their glazed-donut bodies, chocolatey heads, piped-on legs, and candy eyes, these sweet little spiders are sure to be a hit!

Makes 6 donut spiders

1. In a microwave-safe bowl, microwave the chocolate candy melts in 30-second intervals, stirring in between, until melted, about 1 minute total.

2. Insert a toothpick into each donut hole and dip into the melted chocolate until fully coated.

3. Add a donut hole to the center of each donut and let the chocolate harden.

4. Pipe three legs on each side of the donut hole using the tube of black decorating icing.

5. Attach 2 eyes to each donut hole with the remaining decorating icing.

7 ounces chocolate candy melts

6 donut holes

6 glazed donuts

1 tube black decorating icing

12 candy eyes

Halloween Candy Bark

Serves 8

14 ounces melting chocolate

6 Reese's Peanut Butter Cup Minis

¼ cup mini pretzel sticks, broken in half

¼ cup candy corn

¼ cup Reese's Pieces

12 candy eyeballs, plus more for scattering

Halloween sprinkles

1 tube black decorating icing

Halloween memories just got a whole lot sweeter with Halloween Candy Bark. Pour melted chocolate over a baking sheet and customize it with your favorite Halloween candy. To this day, I still love Reese's Peanut Butter Cups, so I had to create a spider by arranging pretzel sticks around Reese's Peanut Butter Cup Minis and adding candy eyes for an extra whimsical touch. From your favorite Halloween candy to candy corn to Reese's Pieces to colorful sprinkles, top your candy bark off with whatever your thoughtful and caring heart desires. Once you've decorated your bark, pop it in the freezer for 1 hour to set. When it's ready, take it out and slice it into bite-size pieces. Be prepared for a cutting challenge, as the bark can be pretty hard straight from the freezer. But don't worry, once the candy bark reaches room temperature, it will have a rich flavor that is slightly chewy and oh-so-chocolaty! Remember, a little goes a long way with this rich and indulgent Halloween treat.

1. Line a large baking sheet with parchment paper. In a microwave-safe bowl, microwave the chocolate in 30-second intervals, stirring in between, until melted, about 1 minute total.

2. Pour the melted chocolate onto the baking sheet and use a spatula to spread the chocolate into an even layer.

3. Working quickly before the chocolate sets, add a mini peanut butter cup for the spider body and 6 half-pretzels for the spider legs. Evenly distribute the candy corn, Reese's Pieces, candy eyeballs, and sprinkles over the rest of the melted chocolate.

4. Using dabs of black decorating icing, attach 2 candy eyes to the top of each peanut butter spider for its eyes.

5. Set the bark in the freezer for 5 to 10 minutes to harden the chocolate. Cut it into smaller pieces.

CELEBRATING TIP

Put your leftover Halloween candy to good use by making Halloween Candy Bark!

Thanksgiving Turkey Cookies

A holiday built around food, family, and gratitude? That's my kind of celebration! In our busy lives, it's easy to lose sight of what truly matters. Thanksgiving is a welcome pause, a time to savor connections and appreciate those small moments. I've always loved how food memories and traditions bring us together. These adorable turkey cookies are a favorite with my kids, Charlie and Claire, and a perfect way to make a new Thanksgiving memory. With leftover Halloween candy corn, Oreos, Reese's Peanut Butter Cups, candy eyeballs, and Reese's Pieces, they're a sweet, memorable treat for the whole family. The days are long, but the years are short—here's to making happy food memories that last!

Makes 12 cookies

12 Oreos

1 tube black decorating icing

12 Reese's Peanut Butter Cup Minis

60 candy corns

6 orange Reese's Pieces

24 candy eyeballs

1. Lay an Oreo flat in front of you for the turkey's body. Use some decorating icing to attach a mini peanut butter cup to the bottom edge of the Oreo that is closest to you for the turkey's head.

2. Now draw a thin bead of icing in an arc along the top edge of the Oreo. Attach 5 candy corns with their pointed side facing inward above the peanut butter cup (these are the turkey feathers).

3. With a knife, cut the Reese's Pieces in half. Use decorating icing to attach a half-piece, cut side down, to the center of each peanut butter cup to form the turkey's beak.

4. With the remaining decorating icing, attach 2 eyes to each peanut butter cup above the beak.

Oreo Cookie Santas

8 ounces (1 cup)
white candy melts

12 golden Oreos

12 red M&M's

6 mini marshmallows

8 ounces (1 cup)
red candy melts

24 mini chocolate chips

Ho-ho-hold on to sweet memories with these Santa cookies. Speaking of Santa and cookies . . . This might be one of the wildest things I've ever done, but five years ago, we surprised the kids on Christmas morning with a red mini Goldendoodle puppy—Hallmark-movie style! We got her all the way from Utah, and I hid her at my parents' house until Christmas morning. Luckily, my parents live only three minutes away, so living a secret double life while waiting to surprise the kids was totally doable. On Christmas morning, my parents came over and snuck in our new puppy wrapped in a box that was already covered with plaid wrapping paper (with plenty of ventilation!). My husband, Andy, placed it under the tree, and out popped little Miss Cookie Sue, who completed our family! I knew the kids would be completely shocked, but they surpassed my expectations, screaming and crying tears of joy! You can see the video on my Instagram @BestFriendsForFrosting. They had been begging for a puppy for nearly four years, and I'd always wanted to do this. You're only little once, and this felt like a once-in-a-lifetime opportunity! What happy holiday memories can you surprise your loved ones with—the kind that will make your face hurt from smiling so big?

Just like that Christmas surprise, these Santa cookies are a sweet treat that's sure to bring smiles. They're perfect for celebrating every day in December, or at Christmas parties, including classroom festivities. These cookies are guaranteed to bring smiles to everyone's faces. Dip half of the Oreo in white chocolate for Santa's fluffy beard, one-third in red candy melts for his jolly hat, and top it off with a marshmallow. Add a red M&M for his rosy nose and chocolate chips for his twinkling eyes. Get ready to sprinkle the sweetest holiday cheer.

1. In a microwave-safe bowl, microwave the white candy melts in 30-second intervals, stirring in between, until melted, about 1 minute total.

recipe continues

CELEBRATING TIP

Start a new family tradition by leaving out Oreo Cookie Santas each year for Santa and his reindeer.

2. Line a baking sheet with parchment paper. Dip half of each Oreo into the white candy melts. Place on the parchment paper and immediately add 1 red M&M in the center for Santa's nose.

3. Slice the mini marshmallows in half and set aside.

4. In another microwave-safe bowl, microwave the red candy melts in 30-second intervals, stirring in between, until melted, about 1 minute total.

5. Dip the top one-third of each Oreo in the red candy melts to resemble Santa's hat. Immediately add a mini marshmallow to the side of the melted red candy to be the tassel at the end of the hat.

6. Use the remaining melted white chocolate to stick on 2 mini chocolate chips for Santa's eyes.

7. Let cool for 20 minutes before serving.

Santa's elves whipped up the CUTEST letter-to-Santa wish-list template just for you! Jingle all the way to **BestFriendsForFrosting.com/FreePrintables** *to download yours.*

WHETHER A QUICK WEEKNIGHT
DINNER OR A SPECIAL HOLIDAY
TREAT, FAMILY RECIPES BECOME
CHERISHED AND NOSTALGIC
REMINDERS OF THE LOVE AND
JOY THAT FILL OUR HOMES

Frosty *the* Snowman Donut Skewers

Bring Frosty to life by adding a piece of baby carrot for his nose and give him some eyes and a smile using mini chocolate chips secured with a drop of frosting. Complete the look by adding M&M's for buttons and tying a Sour Streamer scarf or ribbon in your favorite festive color or pattern—anything pink, polka dot, striped, or gingham for me, please! Whether you're looking for a dessert memory to make with the kids or want to put together a sweet surprise, these Frosty treats are fun for any winter occasion.

*Makes
6 skewers*

1. Thread 3 mini donuts onto each skewer and tie a ribbon or Sour Streamer underneath the top donut.

2. Pipe small beads of decorating icing to adhere 2 red M&M's for the snowman's buttons, 4 mini chocolate chips for the mouth, and 2 mini chocolate chips for the eyes.

3. Insert half a baby carrot into the middle of the top donut for the nose.

18 mini powdered donuts

Six 10-inch wooden skewers

Thin ribbon or thin strips of Haribo Sour Streamers

1 small tube vanilla decorating icing

12 red M&M's

36 mini chocolate chips

3 baby carrots, cut in half

Cranberry Bliss Fudge

Serves 8

Cooking spray

One 14-ounce can sweetened condensed milk

4 cups white chocolate chips

1 teaspoon vanilla extract

1 cup dried cranberries

1 Cuties clementine

One of my first jobs was as a barista at Starbucks. I'll never forget that winter afternoon when I tried my FIRST Cranberry Bliss Bar. Life-changing! IYKYK! I have had the honor of introducing the whole family to this seasonal happy treat. I am always the first person to take my mom, my nieces, and my kids to get their first Cranberry Bliss Bar each year. This recipe transforms the classic Starbucks treat into a creamy, melt-in-your-mouth fudge that's incredibly easy to make and full of big festive flavors.

1. Line an 8 × 8-inch baking dish with parchment paper and grease the paper with cooking spray.

2. In a small microwave-safe bowl, combine the condensed milk and white chocolate chips and microwave in 30-second intervals, stirring in between, until melted.

3. Stir in the vanilla and ¾ cup of the dried cranberries. Pour the mixture into the prepared pan and top with the remaining cranberries. Grate the zest of the clementine over the fudge.

4. Refrigerate for 2 to 3 hours to set. Cut into squares to serve.

ACKNOWLEDGMENTS

To God, who placed this book on my heart and gave me the words to share it.

Andy,
Thank you for supporting my dreams and being my biggest cheerleader! Your beautiful photos and videos inspire millions to create joyful food memories. I'm so proud of your talent and dedication. I'm so grateful we get to balance our family and business together. Most of all, I'm grateful I hit "accept" on that Myspace friend request! Cheers to twenty years, and many more ahead! Love you forever!

Charlie and Claire,
You made me a mama and have completed my whole heart. Thank you for making every day—even ordinary ones—feel so special. You give me purpose and make me smile a mile! I am a better and happier person because of you. You are the greatest blessing and gift of ALL time. What a joy and privilege it is to be your mama! I love you with all my heart!

Mom and Dad,
Thank you for loving me unconditionally and always teaching me I can do anything I put my mind to. Thank you for ALWAYS making every day and holidays so special. I love our memories together. I not only consider you the best parents, but you are both truly two of my very best friends. I love you both so much!

My in-laws,
Thank you for wonderful holidays and for making me feel like part of the family from the start. O'Loughlin Christmases will always hold a special place in my heart.

Team BFFF,
Molly, Kim, and MaryAnn,
BFFF wouldn't have been the same without your friendship, talent, and unwavering support over the years. Thank you for being more than just teammates—you're my BFFFs for life.

My followers,

Thank you for welcoming me into your lives! Your support means everything. Thank you for embracing my enthusiasm, even when I talk a mile a minute! As a fellow celebrator, I'm cheering you on to sprinkle moments of joy within your own four walls at home. When you celebrate the good, the good gets better! Here's to building your legacy of happy family memories! Love you all so much!

My agent and publisher,

To my literary agent, Sharon, and the team at HarperCollins, Sarah and Jacqueline: Thank you for believing in this book from the start! Your support and guidance have been invaluable. I'm excited for this book to make a positive difference in the lives of families to celebrate every day! So much love and gratitude to you all!

INDEX

Note: Page references in *italics* indicate photographs.

ABOUT *the* AUTHOR

Melissa Johnson is the down-to-earth mom next door behind the blog *Best Friends for Frosting,* where she connects with millions of readers by sharing super-easy recipes that transform everyday moments and holidays into cherished memories. Her brand's signature bright and cheerful style has also expanded into happy lifestyle products that celebrate both the everyday and the holidays through the *Best Friends for Frosting* shop.

Melissa's easy recipes and party ideas have attracted attention from notable platforms, including Food Network, *Good Morning America,* Martha Stewart, QVC, Pottery Barn Kids, *Woman's Day,* and Reese Witherspoon.

Now an author, entrepreneur, wife, and mother of two, Melissa lives in sunny Sacramento, California, with her husband, Andy, and their two wonderful children, Charlie and Claire.

Is celebrating your love language? Let's be best friends!
Follow everywhere @BestFriendsForFrosting.

And I would absolutely love for you to join our Facebook group,
"Best Friends for Frosting® CELEBRATORS," at
Facebook.com/groups/BestFriendsForFrosting.
We're a community of memory makers, tradition keepers,
and holiday cheerleaders who will cheer you on!